SONS OF ISSACHAR

FOR THE

21ST CENTURY

...understanding God's heart for our times

Bill Lewis

xulon
PRESS

To my beloved wife, Lynn,
the love of my life
and the greatest gift God has given me,
and our four precious children,
Joshua, Justin, Abby, and Grace.

May the Lord raise us all up
as Sons of Issachar for the 21st century.

"…the sons of Issachar,
who had understanding of the times,
to know what Israel ought to do…."

I Chronicles 12:32 (NKJV)

Table of Contents

In I Chronicles 12:32, David is joined in battle by "the sons of Issachar, who understood the times...." Can God help us to understand the times in which we live? What are the "macro" themes of our age in history? What is the nature of the spiritual battle raging in our day? Does God have a unique and urgent message for our generation? And if so, how should we pray?

God uses us to accomplish His plans. When we pray, we actually participate in what God is doing on earth. Drawing exciting parallels with the book of Exodus, this chapter describes the spiritual significance of the roller-coaster ride that was Election 2000, when a divided nation was given a wake-up call to pray...and keep praying. Through those tumultuous events, God pulled back the curtain and revealed the nature of the spiritual battle of our day. If we are to have any hope of seeing revival and averting judgment, then we, the Body of Christ, must commit ourselves to sustained, fervent prayer. A spiritual battle was won, but the war is still raging over this country...a war that has implications and ramifications for Israel, and for the world in which we live.

Our nation stands at a spiritual, as well as historic, crossroads. Will we experience judgment...or revival? We must seek God in the same spirit as Daniel, a humble man who worshipped, repented, and interceded for his people and nation. "Who knows if he [the Lord] will relent and leave a blessing behind him?" (Joel 2:14). As an example, this chapter also details an inspiring account of how the Puritan settlers sought the Lord in the face of an imminent danger.

The tragic events of September 11, 2001 were a sign that the Church in America is "asleep in the light." This chapter is a passionate plea for fasting, humility, and prayer on behalf of our beloved nation, as well as an exhortation to seek personal revival.

"Stand at the crossroads and look; ask for the ancient paths..." (Jeremiah 6:16). Find out what the Pilgrims and Puritans believed were God's purposes for the new world, and for the nation of Israel. Does God have a "redemptive purpose" for the United States of America?

"Get the rubbish out of the temple!" This message — a word of hope, a call to faith, and a challenge to repentance — draws exciting and inspiring parallels between our generation and that of King Hezekiah, who ushered in the longest revival in Israel's history. A stirring call to renew our covenant with God, to gather the elders of our land for prayer, and to cleanse our hearts.

God has a unique calling for President George W. Bush. He can be used by God like King Hezekiah, who, though a civil leader, led his nation to seek the Lord. And, he can be like Cyrus, the ancient King of Persia who, though not Jewish, was greatly used by God to bless and help the Jewish people.

Does God's covenant with Israel still stand? Is there any significance to the re-establishment of the State of Israel? Or is God finished with the Jewish people? How important is it for the United States to support Israel?

Drawing meaningful parallels from the book of Ruth, this chapter describes the Church's calling — and command — to bless the Jewish people and the nation of Israel. "For this is what the LORD Almighty says:...whoever touches you touches the apple of his eye" (Zech. 2:8).

An historical overview of the tragic way in which the Church has treated the Jewish people throughout history. How can we move toward reconciliation in the Body of Christ between Jew and Gentile? What is the wisest way to present the good news of the Messiah to Jewish people?

God promised Abraham, "I will bless those who bless you, and whoever curses you I will curse" (Genesis 12:3). Was this promise valid only in Biblical history, or does the above Scripture have any relevance for us today? If the promise of Genesis 12:3 is indeed true, then we would expect to find evidence both in Biblical history, and in events taking place since that time as well. Does such evidence exist? What are the ramifications for the nations of the earth, and for the Church in those nations?

What is the real aim of Islam? What does the Koran actually say about *jihad*? This chapter traces the origins and historical facts concerning the militant nature of the Islamic faith.

Is the god of Islam really the same Biblical God of Abraham, Isaac, and Jacob? What is behind the three historic resurgences of Islam? Does the Qur'an really preach respect and tolerance for other religions? Find out about the momentous implications for Christianity and, indeed, for Western civilization.

What kind of person can God use to impact a generation? This chapter casts a vision for America's destiny, and exhorts us to be like Esther, who discovered her unique purpose and position for the day and circumstances in which she lived. If we humble ourselves, pursue God, and seek to "understand the times," then each of us can learn why we were born "for such a time as this."

Acknowledgements

Thank you to my precious wife Lynn, for her abundant encouragement and support, for her help typing and revising the manuscript, and especially for battling with the computer all year.

I would also like to thank the following people who helped this book come into being: Sylvia Burleigh, at Xulon Press, for patiently answering all my questions, Faithe Finley at Master Design for her invaluable advice and encouragement, and Jim and Libby Ladyman, who strongly urged me to write a book.

The Lord has particularly used the following brothers and sisters, as "iron sharpeners," to significantly encourage and assist me along the way: my wise and wonderful parents, Bill and Diane Lewis; also Cindy & Lou Davis, Stan Hays, Bonnie Wallace, Geddes and Holly Self, Lynn and Tawni Ballinger, Mary Quinlan, Larry Crabb, Mark and Melinda Cathey, Tom White, Mary Lance Sisk, Buddy and Sally Jones, Margaret Moberly, Jim Holmes, Kevin Weaver, Marshall and Cindy Meador, Michael Deaderick, who gave me a love for history and what it can teach us, and last but not least, Dr. Gary Cook, who, when I was at Baylor University, challenged me to pursue ministry and told me that I would one day write books.

And most of all, I am grateful to my Lord and Savior, Jesus Christ, my Redeemer and the Restorer of my soul. It is Your constant love and faithfulness that make me yearn to be a son of Issachar.

Introduction

For many years I've been intrigued by the description of the Sons of Issachar in I Chronicles 12:32. Scripture tells us they were men "who understood the times and knew what Israel should do." What an asset such men must have been to King David! If Israel needed such men 3,000 years ago, then surely America stands in need of such men and women today. Sometimes it does indeed seem that we, as Christians, cannot see the forest for the proverbial trees. We are so preoccupied with what is happening immediately in front of us, that we don't see how such events may indeed be part of a much larger picture.

The wisdom that characterized the Sons of Issachar must come to characterize the Church of our generation as well. Otherwise, the consequences could be catastrophic, not only for the American Church, but for the nation and even for Western Civilization as well.

The United States of America stands at a moral and spiritual crossroads — the most significant one in her history. The spiritual decline in our nation over the past forty years is unprecedented. How is it possible that we could have fallen so far so fast? What lies ahead for our nation? Many voices claim that it is already too late; there is no hope for America. In their view, our condition has deteriorated to the point that it is without remedy. Is that true? Have we indeed crossed the Rubicon into the inevitable and irrevocable judgment of God? What is on the heart of God for the United States in this first generation of the 21st century? Is it still possible that a revival and awakening might stem the tide of darkness and transform our nation in ways that are currently beyond our comprehension?

As we look beyond our borders to the Middle East, we witness a conflict that most Americans do not understand. How could the claim to one miniscule slice of the world's geography threaten to engulf the whole world in such intense conflict? Will the future of the Middle East determine the future of the world? How significant is America's relationship with Israel? What role should our nation play in the resolution of this intractable conflict? Does the Lord indeed have His eye on the land and the people of Israel? What will the generation before us bring to the Middle East and how will it affect the rest of the word?

September 11, 2001 changed America forever. None of our lives will ever be the same. On that one tragic day, the door of history swung violently open to a new era, one that will, I believe, be even more dangerous than any which mankind has previously witnessed. Since the Islamic revolution in Iran in 1979, militant Islam has begun an aggressive sweep across the globe. The generation ahead will witness a clash of civilizations and worldviews not seen for 500 years. The United States, and indeed the entire Western world, must awaken to the imminent danger threatening to crash upon its shores. Ours is a generation that will change history forever — one way or the other. As Christians, we cannot afford to hide our heads in the sand and wait for the storm to pass us by.

We do indeed live in momentous times. I truly believe that those alive today have indeed been born "for such a time as this." The question is: will we rise to fulfill our destiny? Or, will we miss the visitation of the Lord? To have a calling is one thing; to fulfill it is another. If the Church is to arise and fulfill her destiny in the heart of God in this hour, she must have the spiritual eyesight of the Sons of Issachar.

If as God's people we humbly cry out for understanding and discernment, what can we expect to hear from our God? Does He have a message for us? What might He be trying to tell us concerning the times in which we live?

Amos 3:7 says, "Surely the Sovereign Lord does nothing without revealing his plan to his servants the prophets." Our God is the same yesterday, today, and forever. If He desired to reveal His purposes to Amos's generation, then He certainly desires to do no less today. Interestingly enough, Amos was not schooled in the school of the prophets. He was merely an ordinary shepherd who heard God's voice and shared God's heart with the people of Israel. I do not make any claim to be a prophet. I am not a pastor, nor a theologian. I am not a scholar, nor an expert on the themes I write about in this book. There are many far more knowledgeable than I, and I am confident they could write a far better book.

What I offer is the testimony of one ordinary man crying out to God for my nation and my people. The Lord called me fifteen years ago to pray for revival and spiritual awakening in America and throughout the world. Every day since then, I have implored the Lord to touch our land once again. As a result, God has revolutionized my life. While I was praying for Election 2000 and its aftermath, the Lord began to speak to my heart a word of hope, a call to faith, and a challenge to repentance — a message that still rings true four years later.

I never planned to write a book. It seemed a daunting task which, in my view, would require far too much work. Many different people who heard me share this message strongly encouraged me to write a book, but I continually rebuffed the suggestion. Then one day the Lord spoke to my heart very clearly through Jeremiah 36:1-3:

> ...this word came to Jeremiah from the Lord: 'Take a scroll and write on it all the words I have spoken to you concerning Israel, Judah and all the other nations from the time I began speaking to you...till now. Perhaps when the people of Judah hear about every disaster I plan to inflict on them, each of them will turn from his wicked way; then I will forgive their wickedness and their sin.'

I have written this book in obedience to the prompting of the Holy Spirit. I submit it to you to take before Lord for testing and confirmation. If its message bears witness with your spirit, I invite you to join me in turning the themes of this book into prayers that I believe reflect God's heart for our nation and our people in this hour. If we pray from of God's heart, we may be assured that He will hear us — and answer us.

Micah son of Moresheth prophesied in the days of Hezekiah king of Judah. He told all the people of Judah, 'This is what the Lord Almighty says: "Zion will be plowed like a field, Jerusalem will become a heap of rubble...."' " Did Hezekiah king of Judah or anyone else in Judah put him to death? Did not Hezekiah fear the Lord and seek his favor? And did not the Lord relent, so that he did not bring the disaster he pronounced against them?

— Jeremiah 26:18-19

CHAPTER ONE

America at the Crossroads

The Lord has a message for His people. It is found in the lyrics of the popular worship song, "Shout to the Lord." The message: "Nothing compares with the promise I have in you." [1] Nothing compares with the promise we have in Jesus. This message is for every person who is in Christ. Nothing compares to the promise and the purpose we have in the heart of God in this generation. What an awesome truth!

Over the past several years God has been teaching me about the promise that we, as His body, have in His purposes. We live in a unique generation. I truly believe that we have a special destiny in the heart and purpose of God for our day. Throughout this book, we will be looking at what it means for us to connect our lives on the "micro" level to the purposes of God on the "macro" level.

SONS OF ISSACHAR

I Chronicles chapter 12 lists the men from various tribes who rallied to the side of David. In the middle of this list, we find a very significant editorial comment concerning the Sons of Issachar. The chronicler describes them as "men who understood the times and knew what Israel should do." (I Chronicles 12:32) As David needed

Sons of Issachar in his day, so the Body of Christ needs Sons of Issachar for the 21st century. To first understand, and then participate in, the grand purpose of God in our generation, we must become like the Sons of Issachar. What does it mean for us as Christians to **understand the times** and know what we should do? Personally, I long for that kind of wisdom and understanding, and I am sure you do as well.

It is my conviction that we cannot obey the Lord and enter into the highest purposes He has for the Church and for this nation **unless we understand this time** and this season in which we have been graced to live. I hope that as we seek to flesh out this theme, the Lord will give us insight into His heart. May He not only speak to us a message of hope, but also stir our hearts to faith, and challenge us to prayer and to action.

WHAT REALLY MATTERS?

In 1988, I visited Israel for the first time. While I was standing on the tel at Megiddo, overlooking the valley of Armageddon, I sensed the Lord asking me this question: *"In light of this place, and what will happen here, what really matters?"*

It was a simple, yet profound awareness, an insight that deeply stirred my heart. I remember answering out loud, "Lord, only Your kingdom matters. Nothing else does."

Through this experience atop Megiddo, the Lord sowed a seed deep in my heart. That seed was a desire to see an awesome revival come to the Church in the United States, and in every nation on the face of the earth. There was birthed in my spirit a burning desire to see the greatest spiritual awakening in the history of the world. Within 10 months of my return from Israel in the spring of '88, that seed had become a call to pray...a call to pray for revival and spiritual awakening.

And the Lord answered my prayer in a most interesting fashion. He moved my wife, Lynn, and me to Russia in 1991. Then in late 1998, He switched gears and moved us to Israel, where we lived for over two years.

Everything that has happened in my life in the last fifteen years has its root in what God spoke to my heart atop Megiddo — that

only the kingdom of the Lord matters. Only Jesus' advance in the hearts of men matters. Nothing else even comes close.

Although I lived outside of the United States for ten years, my heart was never far from home. My earnest desire to pray for revival in this nation has never dampened. Many times I have asked, "Lord, could it be that you would send **a fourth great awakening** to the United States?" We have had three great awakenings, one in the 18th century and two in the 19th. Could it be that the Lord would send a fourth? Many have said that the United States is too far gone. Judgment is standing ominously at the door. Yet, for fifteen years, I have been praying for mercy. An admittedly undeserved mercy, yet still that is my heart cry…and I hope it is yours as well.

Since the year 2000, America has begun to experience some serious shakings, most notably the controversy of Election 2000 and the tragic events of September 11, 2001. In His sovereignty, God permitted both of these events to occur. What, if anything, is His message to us? Does God speak to His people through contemporary events? In a later chapter, we will address September 11th specifically. For now, let us turn our attention to Election 2000. What was God trying to say to the Church and the nation through the 36-day ordeal of November 2000? What does this mean for us today, four years later?

As the year 2000 presidential election approached, the Lord impressed upon me how crucial this particular election was for the future of our country. Many calls to fasting and prayer were sounded in advance of the election. I joined in the spirit of such calls to prayer and began to intercede very intensively, especially as the election approached. The Lord's word to me — and I believe to the Church at large — was, "Watch and pray."

While it may be true that certain people seem to possess a special intercessory giftedness, and some ministries are even devoted entirely to intercessory prayer; nevertheless, as believers we dare not say, "Well, intercession is only for those 'called' to such a ministry." We dare not say that, because Scripturally we are all called to intercede. It was to every one of us that Paul wrote, "Pray without ceasing" (I Thessalonians 5:17 NKJV). The great need of the hour is that prayer would become a virtually involuntary response in our lives, just like breathing out and breathing in. O, that we would pray like that! I believe we can learn to pray like that. We can learn to pray the prayers that are on the heart of God.

The night before the election, I attended a prayer gathering on Mt. Carmel in Haifa, Israel. I had been asked to translate into Russian for the many Russian-speaking Jews who would be present. At the end of the prayer gathering, the pastor called forward a group of visitors who were on a short-term trip from the States. The pastor asked them to pray for the election. As it turned out, every member of the group was from Texas. As they started to pray, I could no longer continue translating. Instead, I began to weep. I felt a prayer burning in my heart. When there was an opportunity, I stood and prayed, "Father, as an American Christian and as a representative for my nation, I want to repent before You for all the sins that our nation and our people have committed. What we have done in straying from our roots has grieved You so deeply. You have every right to give us more of what we deserve, yet I ask You for an undeserved mercy. I beseech You not to give us a leader according to what we deserve, but rather a leader according to mercy. Please send revival and awakening to America again."

GOD USES MEN TO ACHIEVE HIS PURPOSES

Before I relate what happened the following day, I would first like to stress an important point about the relationship between the sovereignty of God and the agency (or actions) of man, in this case in regard to prayer. In Scripture, the sovereignty of God is never divorced from the agency of man. **The purpose of God is not accomplished apart from His chosen image bearers,** whom He has redeemed and called into action by his grace. It is indeed a great mystery, and yet the Lord has chosen to involve us in fulfilling His purposes.

Why? I do not know, because at times I do such a pitiful job. Sometimes, we all do. Nevertheless, that is the mystery of God's ways. I would like to suggest that there are generations that do not get done what is on the heart of God to be accomplished because they are not in tune with God's heart. Frankly, this is a danger for our generation as well, particularly as we look at what our nation and the world face today. We must not err through adherence to an inaccurate understanding of the sovereignty of God that justifies ungodly passivity.

God is indeed sovereign, but at the same time it is God Himself who calls us to prayer. God, in His sovereignty, calls us to faithfulness in prayer so that His promises will be fulfilled and His purposes accomplished. **God involves us in what it is He wants to do.** I believe an ungodly passivity that relies on mental assent to the sovereignty of God is an abomination to the Lord. Why? Because it uses a divine attribute to justify our prayerlessness and faithlessness. We cannot afford to abuse the sovereignty of God by excusing ourselves.

On Election Day 2000, after a season of worship and prayer, a deep peace suddenly settled over me. I looked up to heaven and asked, "Lord, is this peace a confidence that, whatever happens today, You are in control? Or is this peace an assurance that You are going to grant us a leader according to mercy?"

Before I could even finish my prayer, like a lightening bolt into my heart the Holy Spirit spoke clearly and powerfully: *"Stand still and behold the salvation of the Lord."*

I was so stunned that I almost fell out of my chair. The Lord directed my attention to Exodus 14:13, "Do not be afraid. Stand still, and see the salvation of the Lord, which He will accomplish for you today....The Lord will fight for you, and you shall hold your peace." (NKJV)

In this verse we clearly see the sovereign involvement of God, made manifest according to a decree issued in heaven: "The Lord will accomplish salvation for you today." As I read that verse, I sensed the Lord saying, "I have heard your prayers, and the prayers of so many others for mercy, and I have granted your request. I have issued a decree of mercy. Exodus 14 is My word, My will, for the current situation your nation faces. You stand here in Exodus 14, and you meditate on this passage, and you pray from this passage, and you praise from this passage."

God is the one who is going to accomplish the deliverance of Israel; yet note what the Lord then says in Exodus 14:16, "But lift up your rod, and stretch out your hand over the sea and divide it.

And the children of Israel shall go on dry ground through the midst of the sea." (NKJV) The Lord had already said He was going to do it, but **He then involved Moses in the miracle.** Earlier the Lord had told Moses to be still and He would accomplish a great miracle by the moving of His righteous hand, yet in Exodus 14:16 we see the agency of Moses in this deliverance.

How awesome that God would want to use Moses, and **that God would want to use you and me to stretch forth His rod!** What was the rod? The rod of His authority. The rod of His decree issued in heaven. The rod of His mercy which he extended to the children of Israel. Moses obeyed the Lord, and as he did, the seas parted, and the children of Israel crossed the Red Sea on dry land.

What happened next? Exodus 14:23 tells us that the Egyptians pursued the Israelites into the midst of the sea. We can imagine the Israelites asking, "Wait a minute, Lord, what about the miracle? Here come the Egyptians — what are You doing?" Yet Exodus 14:4 reveals that it was God Himself who hardened the heart of Pharaoh. Three times in chapter 14 God says that He brought the Egyptians after the Israelites so that He might gain greater honor for His name. (Exodus 14:4, 17, 18) We must emphasize the fact that the Egyptians could not have pursued Israel if God had not allowed them to do so. Exodus 14:31 clearly says that God brought the Egyptians out against His people so that the Israelites would fear God and believe. Not a passive belief, but Biblical belief. Biblical belief is never passive. Biblical belief is never just mental assent. Biblical belief involves the entrustment of our whole being to the purposes of God as He reveals them to us. O, that we would fear the Lord and believe, that we too might have the opportunity to witness a mighty deliverance for our nation!

THE "EGYPTIANS" AND THE ELECTION

On the evening of Election 2000, I stayed up most of the night in Israel. I laid out Exodus 14 before the Lord and cried out, "Lord, I believe this is Your word from heaven. It's Your decree of mercy. I stretch out my rod, and I join with all the others whom I don't know, whom You are leading to do the same thing." When God speaks to us, He is also speaking to many others. We may not know them. In fact, we may never know until heaven all the people who have been led to pray the very same prayer strategy from the Word of God. We do not need to know them; we just need to know what He tells us and to stand on that.

In obedience I stretched out the Word of God, and watched and prayed. There is probably not one American who does not remember what happened next. First, Florida went to Gore, and then it was declared "undecided" again. Then, it went to George W. Bush, who was then declared the President elect of the United States. I stood in my living room and began to praise the Lord.

But when Florida was taken away from George W. Bush and put back in the "undecided" column once more, I could not believe it. I cried out, "Lord, what is going on? I was sure that You said George W. Bush would be our 'leader according to mercy.'" [2] The Lord said, "Read your Bible; read the second half of Exodus 14." In Exodus 14:23, I read that the Egyptians came after the Israelites in an attempt to snatch the Lord's victory. Then the Lord said, "I have given you Exodus 14 so that you would be prepared for what is happening and would not be afraid, but would know that I am granting deliverance. Stand on the Word of the Lord and stretch forth My rod."

I began to pray according to Exodus 14:24, "During the last watch of the night the Lord looked down from the pillar of fire and cloud at the Egyptian army and threw it into confusion. He made the wheels of their chariots come off so that they had difficulty driving." In addition, I noticed something else that I thought must be very significant. The Lord instructed Moses to stretch out his rod over the sea a second time (14:26-27). Twice in one chapter God commanded Moses to stretch forth his rod. The first time Moses stretched forth his rod pictured intercession based on God's decree of mercy and deliverance. God used Moses to initiate the miracle. Then, the second time that Moses stretched out his rod, God used him to consummate the miracle.

When we are praying, sometimes we don't know where we are in that process. We do not know whether God is calling us to initiate something, or whether we are a part of the consummation of something. The most important principle to remember is this: **As God involved Moses, so God desires to involve us both to initiate**

and to consummate deliverance for our nation at this hour.

Beloved, the Lord has no other plan than us — the Church, His body. He could send angels. He could give a personal testimony. He could appear to everyone, or speak out of a thundercloud, as He did at Meribah. But that is not what He has chosen to do most of the time. The Lord is calling us to stand with him as Moses did. He desires for us to hear the word of the Lord in order to initiate and consummate according to His leading.

In the case of Election 2000, thirty-six days after the controversy ensued, we saw the consummation of the miracle. The decree of mercy the Lord had initiated in heaven was enacted on the earth. For those 36 days, I watched and prayed, standing confidently on the word the Lord had given me from Exodus 14. I heard from many people from all over the world who had also been given Exodus 14 to pray for our nation. God's people prayed, and He brought forth the miracle.

AMERICA AT THE CROSSROADS

Afterwards, while meditating before the Lord, I asked Him about the significance of the 50:50 split of everything in our nation — the Congress, the Senate, even the Presidential vote. The Lord's response was, *"The nation has lost its moorings. It is divided. It is ambivalent and doesn't know which way to go. America is at a crossroads, literally, at this moment. This is the crucial hour. I have heard your prayers and I am releasing mercy, but the Body [of Christ] must deepen and broaden its commitment to worship and prayer, or this will be only a mercy drop that dries on the ground. Only continued prayer will move My hand to bring a sustained outpouring of My Spirit."*

The nation at a crossroads…the crucial hour…deepen and broaden prayer. Most assuredly, God is calling me to deepen my prayer life. And, He is calling you to deepen your prayer life. He is calling us to broaden the prayer movement, calling everyone in our circles of influence to pray. It is imperative that we as believers share this timely message with family members, relatives, friends, neighbors, and coworkers. We must spread the word that now is the hour; this is the day. This is the crucial moment; we are at the crossroads.

Even now, four years later, our nation remains more divided than ever. **We must watch and pray.** We must listen and then intercede; we must hear and heed. The future of the church and the future of this nation depend on it.

I believe the Lord desired to use the intensity of the spiritual battle over the election to catalyze the Church to deepen and broaden the prayer movement. **Through Election 2000, God issued a wake-up call to the Church. A call to watch. A call to pray. A call to fear the Lord.**

ARE WE RESPONDING?

How have we as Christians responded to this wake-up call? As you look back on your response to the election, and even your response to September 11th, how has your life changed? Do you fear God as never before? Are you in awe of God as never before? Do you believe Him to move like never before? God is calling us, like Israel of old, to fear the Lord and believe.

I am convinced that another reason the election battle was so intense is that God wanted George W. Bush to know without a doubt that his victory was from the Lord. It was not the victory of the Republican Party, lawyers, or political advisers. God desires that such a revelation continually humble his heart and intensify his desire to seek the Lord. It is my deep conviction that George W. Bush won that election by one vote — and that vote was God's. One vote — the vote of God — a decree of mercy, and an answer to the prayers of His people. Revelation 5:8 presents a beautiful picture of worship and intercession through the imagery of the harps and bowls. The bowls of incense in heaven are filled with the prayers of the saints. Some initiate, some continue, some consummate, and then what happens? God pours out the bowls to bring about the fulfillment of His purpose. In the battle over the election, I believe God did exactly that!

THE BATTLE CONTINUES

I was out of the country at the time, but friends of mine in the prayer movement in the U.S. said they had never before seen so such prayer mobilized. The Church responded in that moment. And God heard. The bowl was filled, and God poured out his mercy. We must remember, however, that it is only a mercy drop. Unless we press into God like never before, it will surely dry on the ground. Most definitely, **a spiritual battle was won, but the war is still raging over this country.** A war that has implications and ramifications for Israel, and for the world in which we live. These are concerns that will be taken up in later chapters of this book.

Though the Body of Christ rallied in that moment of the election, we have since slacked off. We have pulled back. We have not stayed in that place of intense prayer. But God is calling us to pray without ceasing. The election was indeed a wake-up call for the American Church in regard to prayer, and I am not sure that we have heeded it. I have friends from many countries who visit the United States and do ministry here. It is always interesting for me, as an American Christian, to hear other believers' impressions of the Church in the America. Do you know without exception what each one has said to me? "Bill, the church in America is asleep." Or, "The church is in such a deep slumber." Or most recently, a response that deeply grieved me: "Bill, the church is comatose."

Beloved, I cannot stress enough the seriousness of this hour. God is saying, "Wake up. **Watch and pray.** Listen and intercede. Hear and heed. Respond to me. **Let me involve you in My purposes.**" It is a glorious calling. Jesus has reminded me this year that I have not just been saved *from* something, I have been saved *for* something. What a beautiful facet of the grace of God, that He would want to involve you and me in the fulfillment of His purposes.

The question for us is this: will we confess our selfish indifference? Will we confess our apathy and our complacency? Will we confess an ungodly passivity? What matters more to me — the "micro"-prayer requests on my list (and let me stress, they do matter to Him) or the "macro"-prayer requests that are on the heart of God? We must connect our micro-prayer requests to the macro-prayer requests of God. We must connect our lives, day in and day out, to the purposes of God for our generation. God is calling us to have done with lesser things.

WE NEED THE GIFT OF REPENTANCE

The Lord has shown me this past year that it is His kindness that leads me to repentance. We do not have to be in "overt" sin to be far from His heart. Religious people can have a heart that is far from the heart of God. That can be true at times in my life, and in yours. Things which in and of themselves are good, or perhaps neutral, become sinful when they matter more to me than He does. The greatest mercy the Lord can show us as American believers is to convict us of sin. The greatest kindness He can grant us is the gift of repentance. The greatest grace He can pour out upon us is that which He poured out upon the prophet Isaiah. Isaiah received a revelation of his sinfulness in light of the holiness of God, and as a result, he was completely undone in God's presence. But the Lord then touched Isaiah's lips with a tong from the altar, and he experienced first-hand the mercy of God. The mercies of the Lord are fresh everyday. Praise God! O, that we as believers would see, as Isaiah did, how much we are in need of the mercies of God.

Isaiah became impassioned for God because he tasted something most of us never do. Isaiah was not a wicked man; rather, he was a godly man, a member of the righteous remnant of his day. But, even the godliest of us who have an encounter with the living God are undone. We see the holiness of God. We see our own sinfulness in light of His holiness. We taste of the mercy and grace of God in a way greater than we ever imagined. As a result, our hearts thrill and we respond as Isaiah, "Here am I, send me." We cry out, "Impassion me, Lord, for what impassions You. Impassion me to watch and pray. Impassion me to listen and then join the intercession of Jesus. Impassion me to hear and heed Your voice. Impassion me to want to take hold of that rod and stretch it forth at a moment's notice. Impassion me to pray without ceasing. Impassion me to deepen my prayer life. Impassion me to share the word, calling others to pray."

Beloved, I hope you are both touched and encouraged by the message God continues to speak to us through Exodus 14 and Election 2000. If so, share it with somebody. Help broaden the prayer movement one person at a time. Tell a spouse, tell a friend, tell a coworker that now is the hour. **We are at the crossroads even now. We must watch and pray.**

Will we rise up in response to the call of God? Will we have done with lesser things? Will we sacrifice "all the vain things that charm us most," to the blood of Jesus? God is calling us to sacrifice all the lesser things in our lives to the blood of Jesus. O, men and women of God, may we rise up and have done with lesser things. May we, as the hymn says, "give heart and soul and mind and strength, to serve the King of Kings."

A PRAYER IN RESPONSE

Gracious Heavenly Father, with humble hearts we joyfully acknowledge that nothing compares to the promise we have in You. Perhaps we have lost heart. Perhaps we have lost sight of that; sometimes we do. Remind us afresh that nothing compares with you. O, Lord Jesus, like the song says, please be the center of our lives. Be our source; be our light. Be the fire in our hearts and the wind in our sails as we seek to follow You. Would You, alone, be the reason that we live.[3] Jesus,

> *...be our vision. May naught be all else to us, save that Thou art. Thou our best thought by day or by night, waking or sleeping, Thy presence our light. Riches we heed not, nor man's empty praise, Thou our inheritance, now and always, Thou and Thou only, first in our hearts, high King of heaven, our treasure, Thou art.[4]*

Father, may we respond to You. May we respond to the glory and the wonder of the promise that You have for us, individually and corporately as the Church in our nation. May we respond with humility, brokenness, and confession of sin. May we thrill to the truth that You would want to use us and involve us in Your purposes. Lord, would You pour out a spirit of intercession on the Church, and especially on every person who reads this book. Impassion us with a desire to watch and pray, to listen and inter-cede, to hear and heed. May we be rod-bearers as Moses was, stretching forth Your rod in cooperation with You. Fulfill the plan You have for this generation that stretches before us. Father, be glorified in and through us in this hour, for the sake of Jesus. Amen.

CHAPTER TWO

Standing in the Gap in the Spirit of Daniel, Part I

And I will bless Your name
I will give you all my praise
For the finest hour of history...
I can't help but worship You for all You've done.

— Kim Hill [5]

The finest hour in all of history is the hour when Jesus Christ died on the cross for all mankind. The finest hour in my personal history is when I embraced Jesus as my Savior and Lord. By His grace I have been journeying with Him, and I pray will continue to journey with Him all the days of my life, until I go or He comes. It is because of that finest hour, that greatest of *"kairos"* moments, that all others have been made possible. There have indeed been many in kingdom history; from the time of Jesus to the present day. I believe with all my heart that we are living right now in a *"kairos* moment," one more significant than any we have seen for a long time.

In the previous chapter, I focused on the miracle that God extended to us through the results of Election 2000. A decree of mercy was issued from heaven, and then enacted on earth through the prayers of His saints. I suggested that our response should be to fear the Lord and to believe. Not a passive belief, but an active belief based on the conviction that we have been saved not just *from* something in that finest hour when Jesus died, but we have been saved *for* something in this significant hour in which we live. **We have been saved to cooperate with our sovereign Lord and Redeemer in the fulfillment of the plan of the ages;** a plan that transcends every generation and yet links each to the one before it, and to the one after it. **That, I hope, is our goal: to cooperate with the Lord in this** *kairos* **moment in the generation that lies ahead of us.**

AT THE CROSSROADS: THE EXODUS GENERATION

The people of God have found themselves in crossroads moments countless times throughout history. Many of those crossroads moments, or crossroads generations, are recorded for us in Scripture. One such moment involved the Exodus of the children of Israel from Egypt. Afterwards, Moses led the children of Israel to Mount Sinai. While Moses ascended Mt. Sinai to receive the Law of God, the children of Israel were encamped at the foot of the mountain. As God called the nation to a spiritual awakening, the people faced a choice: Do we go forward with God? Or do we go back to Egypt, and all that it symbolizes: sin, idolatry, and worldliness?

We know the choice the Israelites made in that moment. They constructed the golden calf, and they worshipped it. Moses was still in the presence of the Lord, as the children of Israel descended into idolatry. The Lord told Moses what had happened and then said, "I have seen these people, ...and they are a stiff-necked people. Now leave me alone so that my anger may burn against them and that I may destroy them. Then I will make <u>you</u> into a great nation." (Exodus 32:9-10) [Emphasis Added] Moses, the man of God that he was, pleaded with the Lord, "O Lord, ...why should your anger burn against your people, whom you brought out of the land of Egypt with great power and a mighty hand?…Turn from your fierce anger; relent and do not bring disaster on your people." (Exodus 32:11-12)

Exodus 32:14 records that in response to the intercession of Moses, "… **the LORD relented and did not bring on his people the disaster he had threatened.**" What a fascinating scripture! Of this very same incident Psalm 106:23 says, **"So he said he would destroy them — had not Moses, his chosen one, stood in the breach before him to keep his wrath from destroying them."** [Emphasis added]

In the last chapter, I discussed how we might better understand the relationship between the sovereignty of God and the agency of image-bearers. I will not repeat myself here other than to say that we should let Scripture speak for itself in Exodus 32:14 and Psalm 106:23. **And what Scripture says is that the Lord would have destroyed the Israelites had not his intercessor stood in the gap and cried out for mercy.**

AT THE CROSSROADS: THE HEZEKIAH GENERATION

We find another example of a crossroads generation during the reign of godly King Hezekiah. Jeremiah wrote,

> Micah of Moresheth prophesied in the days of Hezekiah king of Judah. He told all the people of Judah, 'This is what the Lord Almighty says: " 'Zion will be plowed like a field, Jerusalem will become a heap of rubble, the temple hill a mound overgrown with thickets.' " Did Hezekiah king of Judah or anyone else in Judah put him to death? Did not Hezekiah fear the LORD and seek his favor? **And did not the LORD relent, so that he did not bring the disaster he pronounced against them?** (Jeremiah 26:18-19) [Emphasis added]

Hezekiah feared the Lord and sought His favor. As a result, **the Lord relented.** Hezekiah's generation saw not judgment, but arguably the greatest revival and awakening in the history of the kingdoms of Israel and Judah.

AT THE CROSSROADS: THE EZEKIEL 22:30 GENERATION

Yet another crossroads moment is found in the twilight of Judah's history. Nebuchadnezzar, the king of Babylon, destroyed Jerusalem and carried the survivors into captivity. It is of this period that the Lord utters these words, perhaps among the saddest in all of Scripture: " *'I looked for a man among them who would build up the wall and stand before Me in the gap on behalf of the land so I would not have to destroy it, but I found none. So I will pour out my wrath on them and consume them with my fiery anger, bringing down on their own heads all they have done,' declares the Sovereign LORD."* (Ezekiel 22:30-31)

AT THE CROSSROADS: OUR OWN GENERATION

Today, we, as a church, and as a nation, find ourselves at the crossroads. Like the children of Israel before Mt. Sinai, the people of Judah in the days of King Hezekiah, and the people of Judah in the days of King Zedekiah, we face a critical question. Will we successfully navigate this crossroads, and thereby enter into the revival and awakening that God desires to send us? Or, will we refuse to heed the word of the Lord and incur judgment?

IN THE SPIRIT OF DANIEL

God is saying to us, "Rise up! Rise up as watchmen and stand in the gap. Stand on behalf of the Church and the nation, in the spirit of Daniel."

In this chapter, we have seen from Scripture that when the intercessors rose up, God relented! God had mercy. That is what I long to see today in our nation that I love so much, one that in the past has been a bright light for the Gospel.

But why Daniel? Why do I say that we need to stand "in the spirit of Daniel"? What is it that characterized his life as an intercessor? What would it mean for us to be like Daniel, and to stand in the gap as he did?

DANIEL WORSHIPPED

First of all, Daniel was a **worshipper.** During the reign of King

Darius, Daniel worshipped God even at the risk of his own life. Daniel's enemies had tricked Darius into issuing a decree that anyone who worshipped a god other than King Darius during a period of 30 days would be put to death. Even though he had heard about the decree, Daniel, as was his habit, opened his windows to Jerusalem and worshipped God three times a day. What an amazing testimony!

Daniel had the heart of a worshipper. Daniel's challenge to us is this: **what do we worship three times a day?** What do we open our windows and choose to gaze upon? Who — or what — is getting your worship today? We can sit in a Sunday school class and not worship God. We can attend a Bible study and not worship God. We can even go through the forms of "worship" and still not worship God. The Lord said, "These people come near to me with their mouth and honor me with their lips, but their hearts are far from me...." (Isaiah 29:13) Christian forms and rituals mean nothing to the Lord if our hearts are not in them. Do I — do you — have the heart of a worshipper? What is the bent of your heart? Where is your heart inclined today?

DANIEL CONSECRATED HIMSELF

Secondly, Daniel chose to **separate himself from pagan influences**, but not from the pagans themselves. Daniel purposed not to defile himself with the king's food, which would have been sacrificed to idols. Instead, he and his friends asked for fruit, vegetables, and water. At the end of the trial period, Daniel and his friends were healthier than all the others.

Daniel lived most of his life among the pagans of Babylon and Persia. God even raised him up to a place of influence in these kingdoms. Yet, unfortunately, it seems that in modern Christian America, we have tended to do the opposite: **We have insulated ourselves from the pagans, from the unbelievers, but pagan influences often permeate the Church as much as they do secular society.** Beloved, this should not be!

Daniel refused to be defiled by the influences of the cultures in which he lived, yet he remained among the people of those cultures. Likewise, we too should be out among the unbelievers and not allow ourselves to be insulated by the Christian subculture.

DANIEL HUMBLED HIMSELF

Thirdly, Daniel, being grieved and broken by the state of his people, **humbled himself** before the Lord. (Daniel 9:2-3, 10:2-3) Daniel was heartbroken because he saw a people that had refused to heed God's warnings, and as a result, had been taken into captivity for 70 years. In his grief, Daniel stood in the gap. He sought to repair the breach, crying out for God to have mercy on His people and restore them. **Daniel was grieved above all else by the sad spiritual state of his own people.**

What grieves our hearts? What is it that breaks your heart? Is it what grieves God's heart? Is your heart broken by what breaks His heart? May the Lord grieve our hearts with what grieves His heart. May the Lord break our hearts with what breaks His! When we allow ourselves to be broken, we allow God to use our hearts to feel His pain. That is the role of an intercessor. An intercessor makes himself available to God, so that God can pour through him the grief that is on the heart of God. The intercessor then reflects God's heart back to Him. God has so ordained that this type of intercessory prayer moves the hand of God. That is what Moses, Hezekiah, and Daniel did. They all stood in the gap, and God poured out His mercy.

DANIEL CONFESSED HIS OWN SIN

Fourthly, Daniel **confessed his own sins.** Throughout Daniel chapter 9, Daniel talks about sin again and again. Sin, failure, disobedience, and turning from the God of his fathers. Personal confession is the place to start if we want to see God stir the Church. If I want to see God move in the Body, then I must be willing to have Him move in me first. If I want to see God awaken this nation, I must be willing to be awakened. If I want to see other people repent, I must repent. It begins with me! And, it begins with you. Revival begins one heart at a time — one broken heart at a time. God can use one broken heart to kindle another broken heart. And before we know it, God can move corporately by His Spirit to give the gift of brokenness and humility, and then to pour out His mercy.

If we want to be like Daniel, we must ask, "Lord, where have I failed You?" Would you dare to pray that? "Lord, where am I failing You?" Most of us are afraid to pray such a prayer. In 1985, I began to pray, "God, show me that by nature I am a creature of wrath." I had known the Lord since I was a child, but I did not think that I could see the sinfulness of my heart as I needed to see it. At the time a dear friend of mine said, "Oh, Bill, if you pray that, God will show you!"

And beloved, He did! And He has! And He is! But I have found that **it is the most liberating experience to be undone in the presence of God!** To let the Holy Spirit speak to me about things that I need to repent of! Do you know why it is liberating? Do you know why I am not afraid? Because God does not condemn me! Today many of us are afraid to confess to God what we would be afraid to confess to man, because we have <u>all</u> been condemned by man before. We have felt condemnation from someone, be it from parents, peers, preachers, or teachers. Our experience has taught us that exposure is something we must guard against at all costs! **But, when we guard against exposure in the presence of God, we numb ourselves to His heart!** There is no way that you or I can taste personally of the riches of the mercy and grace of God unless we are willing to be exposed in His presence.

I can testify from personal experience that God is good! Yes, He is the Righteous Judge, but He is also the perfect Heavenly Father. He is our *Abba*. When we are willing to be undone in His presence and say, "God, where have I failed You?", then He lovingly shows us. He wraps us in His warm embrace. He gathers us to Himself. **In sensing His unconditional love and acceptance, we come to know what mercy is because we know we do not deserve it. We come to know grace in a fresh way.** Then, something happens — and it is a spiritual mystery in our hearts — we become compelled by the grace of God. We are constrained by the love of God. We want to love Him! We want to worship like Daniel did! **We want to repent again! "Lord, show me something else!"**

The Lord has taught me that such an encounter with Him is not a one-time experience. Instead, <u>**life is about continually embracing the Gospel.**</u> We embrace the Gospel the first time to be saved from the penalty of sin. But from that point on, as we journey with the Lord, we must continually embrace the Gospel in order to be transformed and restored as redeemed image-bearers. As we do so, we too, like Daniel, can be a part of the purpose and plan of God for the generation in which we live.

Several things are true of every person on the face of this planet. First of all, every person is a creature of dignity. Every person — every man and every woman — is made in the image of God. Each one of us has a destiny in the heart of God! Individually and corporately, we have a destiny — we are living in a *kairos* moment. May we make the most of it by God's grace.

Secondly, we have all been marred by sin. Not one of us is unstained by the destructive power of sin. Thirdly, all who know Jesus Christ as their personal Savior and Lord have been redeemed by mercy and grace. Fourthly, God wants to restore us. He wants to restore the image of Jesus in us, but He can only do it in His presence. **He can only do it if we are willing to be undone, broken, and to see the truth**. However, I can guarantee you: God will not condemn you. God will *convict* you, but He will not condemn you. So, beloved, let us press into the Lord. You may fear to expose your innermost self to another, but do not fear to expose your soul before Him! If we refuse to open our hearts up to Him, we refuse the mercy and grace of God. We refuse the healing touch of Jesus.

Lastly, as we are being restored, God wants to use each of us to fulfill a unique and holy purpose. We are all "divine originals," and the Lord has a special purpose for each of us. May the Lord show us our pitiful idolatries. May He reveal our petty idols for what they are: lifeless wood and stone that numb our hearts to the touch of the living God. Only then can we begin to move into the destiny we have in Him in our generation.

DANIEL CONFESSED SIN ON BEHALF OF HIS PEOPLE

The fifth observation about Daniel as an intercessor is that he also confessed the sin of his people. Not only did he confess his own personal sin, but he also **identified himself with the sins of his people and his fathers.** This type of prayer has now come to be known as **"identificational repentance."** In identificational repentance, an individual believer identifies himself with the sins of his family, perhaps, or the sins of the Church, or his nation, and confesses them before God. Daniel, Ezra, and Nehemiah are all

Biblical examples of men who identified with the sins of their people and asked for forgiveness, even though they had not participated in the sinful acts themselves. (Ezra 9; Nehemiah 1; Daniel 9) Why is such repentance necessary?

BREAKING CURSES RESULTING FROM UNCONFESSED SIN

We know from Deuteronomy 27 and 28 that where sin goes, cursing goes as well. Where sin drives its stake into the ground, the consequences come home to roost. Consequences that can affect the Church, a nation, or an ethnic group. Biblically, blessings accompany obedience, and curses accompany disobedience. As Americans and as Christians, we can move redemptively to confess not only <u>our</u> sins, but also the sins of our people, just as Daniel did. The Bible presents Daniel as a righteous man. Why, then, was he confessing the sins of his people? Because he wanted to see the removal of the curse that was affecting his people at that time. He wanted to see God pour out His Spirit in mercy, renewal, and restoration. "If <u>my</u> people, who are called by my name, will humble themselves and pray and seek my face and turn from their wicked ways, then will I hear from heaven!" There is no doubt. "[I will] hear from heaven and will forgive their sin and will heal their land." (II Chronicles 7:14) The Church needs this healing! And, our nation desperately needs it as well.

As Christians, dare we ask, "Lord, where have we, as the Body of Christ, failed You? Not just where have <u>I</u> failed You, but where have we as the Body failed you? Where have we, as Americans, as an ethnic group, as a nation, as a people, failed You?" What have our idolatry, materialism, spiritual apathy, complacency, disunity, personal kingdom-building (whether it be our financial kingdoms or our ministry kingdoms), prayerlessness and lovelessness done to the heart of God? **What damage have our sins done to the spiritual wall of the Church?** What damage have we done to the spiritual wall of our nation? As believers in Jesus Christ, we are the only ones that God can use to repair the breach.

I will share my reflections about the events of September 11, 2001 in a later chapter. For now, let me say that the tragic events of

September 11th were only possible because there are holes in our walls, beloved. There are horrible breaches in the spiritual wall of this nation. The situation facing our nation will not improve; it will only worsen unless we step up into the gap like Daniel, in humility and brokenness, and plead for mercy. Then, I believe such mercy will come in abundance.

HISTORICAL PRECEDENT: THE 17TH CENTURY PURITANS

You may ask if we have an example of the application of the above principles in our own history. Is there a time in our nation's history when American Christians have done this? When they have faced a threat because of the removal of the blessing of God from their land? When they have turned to Him, and seen God bring renewal? The answer is yes. We find an excellent example during the era of the Pilgrims and the Puritans.

We will examine the contribution of the Pilgrims and the Puritans to our country in greater depth in a later chapter. For now, I would like to note that God used them in a very significant way to plant a righteous root in our nation. Yet, over the course of a generation or two, the Puritans' fire dampened. As Puritan scholar, Cotton Mather, put it, **"Religion begat prosperity, and the daughter devoured the mother."** [6] As God's blessing was withdrawn from the Massachusetts Colony, a very severe Indian uprising erupted in 1675. Dr. Peter Marshall, noted expert on the Christian roots of our nation, describes what happened in his book, <u>The Light and the Glory</u>:[7]

> There was one way in which God's blast of judgment might descend on a complacent, greedy, self-oriented people which was so ominous that no one dared think about it, let alone put it into words: a general, coordinated Indian uprising.

[In our day we are experiencing a terrorist uprising, are we not? As you read this account, think of the parallels to what is occurring in America and the world today.]

New England was totally unprepared, strategically, mentally, and spiritually. A company of local militia would be hastily called out and dispatched to the relief of a beleaguered town or hamlet, only to be cut to pieces by a well-placed ambush waiting for it. A second column would be sent to the aid of the first, only to blunder into another ambush set for it. And so it went, until the settlers were afraid to go into the woods, let alone vigorously pursue the enemy. Throughout New England, morale had sunk to its nadir....Almost immediately a fast day was declared in Massachusetts, but no sooner had the service ended, than reports of fresh disasters arrived. Clearly this time God's wrath was not going to be turned aside by one day's worth of repentance....It was manifestly clear that God was not going to be satisfied with superficial or temporary change. What He now demanded was what He had been calling for all along: nothing less than a complete amendment of life. This would necessitate a rooting out of sin and a dealing with it to a degree which had not been seen on the eastern coast of America for nearly fifty years. At first, the people, frightened and badly shaken though they were, still did not take... [their ministers' cries for repentance] seriously....But the war news got steadily worse. And it was war now, there was no question about that; practically every Indian tribe in New England had donned war paint and was collecting scalps.

Finally, the people began to heed their ministers. The Bay Colony's churches filled, and people who had not attended church in years stood in the aisles and joined in the prayers. For the battle was a spiritual one...even the most pragmatic among them was coming to accept that. God's patience with the colonists' hypocritical ways had come to an end. He was not about to relent and restore the saving grace, which had so long protected them and which they had so long taken for granted, unless the whole fledgling nation had a change of heart....

Not in twenty years had [Puritan leader] Increase Mather preached so often to such capacity crowds. And for the first time in even longer than that, people were listening to every word — not just hearing but heeding. In the face of the repeated successes of the Indians, the much-vaunted Yankee reliance and self-confidence melted away like a candle on a hot stove. A great many farmers...knew the taste of fear for the first time in their lives, and got down on their knees, some of them also for the first time. By April of 1676, there was scarcely a man or woman in all of New England who was not diligently searching his or her own soul for unconfessed or unrepented sin. In fact, it became unpatriotic not to do so as if one were not doing one's part for the war effort....And it was a time for churches to renew their covenants. As one pastor put it. 'We intend, God willing...solemnly to renew our covenant...according to the example in Ezra's time....This is a time wherein the Providence of God does, in a knocking and terrible manner, call for it....'

So many people had sincerely and publicly repented of their ways, so many lives were truly reformed, so many broken relationships were restored, and so many churches solemnly renewed their covenants, that God relented and poured out His mercy. There was a freshness in the colonies, a sense of cleanness, and new hope. The colonies were united in a common cause, while Satan's house divided against itself....Now "luck" seemed to be running so much against the Indians that they began giving themselves up, in small bands, and then in droves.

As quickly as the uprising had erupted, it dissipated, and the decisive victory was won that August of 1676. What a testimony to the power of repentant prayer! May we respond to our current national crisis with the same spirit as our Puritan forebears. As we do so, may the Lord grant us the same mercy as well.

"If my people, who are called by name, will humble themselves and pray and seek my face and turn from their wicked ways, then will I hear from heaven and will forgive their sin and will heal their land." (II Chronicles 7:14)

A PRAYER IN RESPONSE

Beloved, let us bombard the heavens with the prayer of Daniel, that the Lord may relent and shower fresh mercies upon us:

"O Lord, great and awesome God, who keeps his covenant of mercy with those who love him, and with those who keep his commandments, we have sinned and committed iniquity, we have done wickedly and rebelled....O Lord, righteousness belongs to you, but to us shame of face...because of the unfaithfulness which [we] have committed against you. O Lord, to us belong shame of face, to our kings, our princes, and our fathers, because we have sinned against you. To the LORD our God belong mercy and forgiveness, though we have rebelled against him."

"...O Lord our God, who brought your people out of the land of Egypt with a mighty hand,...we have sinned, we have done wickedly! O Lord, according to all your righteousness, I pray, [we pray], let your anger and your fury be turned away from [our cities, and from our nation]....Now therefore, our God, hear the prayer of your servant[s], and [our] supplication[s], and for the Lord's sake cause your face to shine on your sanctuary.... O my God, incline your ear and hear; open your eyes and see our desolations, and the city which is called by your name; for we do not present our supplications before you because of our righteous deeds, but because of Your great mercies. **O Lord, hear! O Lord, forgive! O Lord, listen and act! Do not delay, for your own sake, my God, for your city and your people are called by Your name."** (Daniel 9:4-5, 7-9, 15-19 NKJV) [Emphasis added]

Father, as we ponder the godly example of Daniel, we ask You to change us by Your Spirit. For indeed, You alone can change us. Make us 21st century Daniels. May we commit to meditate on Daniel 9, and to pray it to You over and over again, bombarding the heavens until You relent and pour out Your mercy on our "Judah." For Your mercies are new every morning. Thank You for the beauties of Your mercy and grace, and for the sweet, precious name of Jesus. Amen.

CHAPTER THREE

Standing in the Gap in the Spirit of Daniel, Part II

In the previous chapter we began a look at several characteristics of a "prayer profile" of Daniel. We now turn our attention to **the life of Daniel as he stood in the gap for his people and his nation.** We will examine Daniel's life against the backdrop of what is happening in our nation today. What can we learn from Daniel that will help us face life in a post-September 11th world?

DANIEL WAS AN ORDINARY MAN

When we study the life of Daniel, or any other hero of epic — or, perhaps I should say, Biblical — proportions, I think that we as Christians tend to get intimidated. We look at inscripturated heroes, and think, "How awesome these men and women were in their generations." In one sense, that is true, and yet in another, it is not. Why do I say that? Because **Daniel was just a man.** Daniel observed horrific things in his life. He was among those taken captive to Babylon in 606-605 BC during the first deportation. While in exile, he heard the news of the destruction of Jerusalem. He then lived his entire life in exile. Imagine what it would have been like for him, as a young man, to be taken into exile and then later hear the news that his country was no more. **Daniel was indeed an ordinary man, but he had an extraordinary God. That is the key.** The temptation for us is to look at heroes like Daniel and think that God could never use us as He used them, when in reality that is what God wants for us! We are humans, living in a particular generation, just as Daniel was a human being, living in a particular generation. Yes, he was inscripturated into the Biblical Hall of Fame, and we are no longer writing Biblical history. But, kingdom history is still being written. What will God's kingdom history textbook say about our generation? About the Church of this generation? And more specifically, about my involvement and yours in God's purposes for this hour?

SEPTEMBER 11, 2001

September the 11th, 2001 changed our nation, and the world, forever. We will never be the same. I hope the Church will never be the same. We have viewed something horrific, as did Daniel in 606-605 BC. I spent the thirteen years prior to 9/11 praying for revival in the Church, and for a spiritual awakening in this nation. Thirteen years crying out to God for mercy, crying out to God that the Church would turn to the Lord with an impassioned, fiery heart. Thirteen years praying that an event like that which took place on September the 11th would never happen.

Yet then, as the Lord would have it, I found myself right in the middle of it. September 11, 2001 found me in Washington, DC, in a Senate office building right next to the Capitol, watching everything unfold on Tennessee Senator William Frist's television set. I was evacuated with the staff and stood in front of the Capitol along with congressmen, senators, and journalists — all of whom were in shock. I saw the Chaplain of the Senate praying with a crowd of people circled about him. People's faces registered shock, fear, and disbelief. How could this be happening?

Then came the second wave of panic. "Get away from the Capitol!" yelled the policemen. "There may be a plane headed this way. Go! *Run!*" Swarms of people began running away from the building. Police and fire sirens sounded continually. All planes were grounded, and then the skies fell silent, except for the F-16s patrolling the skies. Later that day, I stood on the balcony of the apartment where I was staying and watched the smoke still rising from the Pentagon. The next day, as I walked the streets, a burnt smell still hung in the air.

I had come to Washington, DC to meet with Christian leaders, in order to discuss prayer strategies for America and for Israel. At the same time, however, I had another assignment from the Lord. I had come to confess my sins and to confess the sins of my people. To fast and to pray. To implore the Lord to have mercy on us.

NOT AT OUR POST

Falling buildings; collapsing walls. What did it all mean? In the days after September the 11th, I continually pondered that question.

The Sunday after the attacks, I attended a church on Capitol Hill. At the end of the service, I knelt at the altar and began to weep. I sobbed wordless prayers and cries for mercy. As I knelt there, I had an experience that may seem a little strange, or perhaps a bit unusual. Perhaps we should not consider it to be strange or unusual, given that our God does not like to be put in a box, and given the fact that God, in Scripture, speaks to His people in many ways.

As I knelt at the altar, in my mind's eye I saw an instant replay, as it were, of the events of 9/11. I saw the planes hit the World Trade Center Towers, and then watched them collapse. I then saw the plane hit the Pentagon, and a large section of the wall collapse. The Lord kept showing me the same pictures again and again. Each time I saw those buildings fall and that wall collapse, I wept still harder and harder. Then, the Holy Spirit spoke to my heart, **"The physical ruins picture the spiritual ruin of the nation. America is in spiritual ruins, ruins of your own making. What you have seen over and over pictures the devastation in the spiritual wall of the capital, Washington, DC, and the nation."**

"Ruins of your own making." What did the Lord mean, "ruins of your own making?" As I pondered that question, the Lord showed me another picture: that of an ancient city wall. I saw the posts for the watchmen all along the walls. Most of those posts were empty. There were a few watchmen in place, but most of the people on the wall were distracted and busy. Many were as children, running around and playing. As I witnessed this scene, the Holy Spirit spoke these words: **"My children are minding their own business, not Mine. My children are playing."**

Of course, there is a place for play. There is a time for leisure and rest. But, as the Church in America today, the question we must ask is, "Have we become more lovers of pleasure than lovers of God?" More lovers of entertainment than lovers of the kingdom? Has the vision of the Lord dimmed in our eyes in light of the things of the world that surround and threaten to engulf us?

DANIEL FASTED FOR HIS PEOPLE

Daniel was not into minding his own business; he was into God's business. Daniel did not play; he mourned. Daniel understood the times and knew what to do — press into God in a spirit of fasting and prayer.

The words of the prophet Joel echo powerfully in our day:

> 'Now therefore,' says the LORD, 'turn to me with all your heart, with fasting, with weeping, and with mourning.' So rend your heart and not your garments; return to the LORD your God, for he is gracious and merciful, slow to anger and of great kindness; and he relents from doing harm. Who knows if he will turn and relent *[as in the days of Moses and Hezekiah],* and leave a blessing behind him? ... Blow the trumpet in Zion *[and in Washington, DC and in every city throughout the land],* consecrate a fast, call a sacred assembly; gather the people, sanctify the congregation. Assemble the elders, gather the children and nursing babes; let the bridegroom go out from his chamber, and the bride from her dressing room. Let the priests, who minister to the Lord, weep between the porch and the altar; let them say, 'Spare your people, O LORD.' (Joel 2:12-17 NKJV)

Fasting is a lost discipline in the modern church. I do not ever remember hearing even one sermon on fasting in my entire life. Fasting may have become a lost art, but now is the time to rediscover it. God is calling the Body to fast and to pray, to mourn and to weep. We dare not refuse to heed His call. We would do so at the risk of grave peril such as this nation has never known.

The only way to learn to fast is to begin to fast. We learn to pray by praying; likewise, we learn to fast by fasting. This is not a book on the fundamentals of fasting. My purpose is to both challenge and encourage you to heed the Lord's call to fast and pray. For more practical information concerning fasting, I encourage the reader to consult <u>The Coming World Revival</u> and <u>7 Basic Steps to Successful Fasting and Prayer</u> by Dr. Bill Bright and <u>The Beginner's Guide to Fasting</u> by Elmer Towns.[8]

DANIEL PLED FOR MERCY FOR HIS PEOPLE

Daniel also pled for mercy. Listen to the heart of Daniel's prayer; it is almost as if he is responding to the word of Joel:

> O LORD, according to all your righteousness, I pray, let Your anger and Your fury be turned away from your city....Now therefore, our God, hear the prayer of Your servant, and his supplications, and for the Lord's sake cause Your face to shine on Your sanctuary....O my God, incline Your ear and hear; open Your eyes and see our desolations and the city which is called by Your name; for we do not present our supplications before you because of our righteous deeds, but because of Your great mercies. O Lord hear! O Lord, forgive! O Lord, listen and act! Do not delay for Your own sake, my God, for Your city and Your people are called by Your name. (Daniel 9:16-19 NKJV)

DANIEL GRIEVED FOR HIS PEOPLE

Daniel's heart cry is similar to Joel's: "Let them say, 'Spare your people, O LORD.' " (Joel 2:17) I believe with all my heart that God is calling the Church in the U.S. into a season of mourning and godly grief. Not a grief without hope, but a deep brokenness and sadness as we look at the spiritual ruin of our land. Our spiritual walls have been breached, and the enemy is plundering. Yet if we will press into the Lord, and fast and pray as Daniel did, I truly believe we will touch the heart of God, and He will relent once again. God is merciful. God hears the cries of the penitent for mercy. That is why the grief that I experience for the Church and for my nation is not a grief without hope, because I know who my God is.

DANIEL INTERCEDED ACCORDING TO GOD'S LEADING

Daniel continually pressed into God in a spirit of fasting and prayer. Throughout the book of Daniel we read about how he received a revelation of God's heart and God's purposes (Daniel 2, 4, 5, 9-11). Throughout the whole book, God continually speaks to Daniel. Daniel himself says in chapter 2:28, "There is a God in heaven who reveals secrets...." Amazing! We have a God in heaven who reveals secrets. A God in heaven who will reveal His counsel. A God in heaven who will reveal to us how to pray. A God in heaven who will show us how we can take part, even in a small way, in the intercession of Jesus in a given hour in our nation's history.

While I was in Washington DC, I visited the White House many times before the attacks on September the 11th. Each time, I went to pray that George W. Bush would enter into the fullness of the calling that God has on his life. One day as I was sitting in Lafayette Park in front of the White House, I had a vision. I saw a commercial jetliner crash into the White House and blow it up. Stunned, I gasped, "Lord, terrorists could crash a plane into the White House!" Immediately I began to pray, crying out to the Lord for mercy over our President and protection for the White House.

A few days later, while once again at the White House, I had another vision. This time I saw a terrorist with a shoulder missile-launcher fire a missile and blow Air Force One out of the sky. Once again, I began to pray that God would have mercy on George W. Bush, protecting him from any harm. After the attacks of September the 11th, I thought, "Lord, could it have been that the White House and Air Force One were also intended targets?" When I mentioned this possibility to some friends, they replied, "Perhaps the Lord was leading you how to pray, because He wished to extend His mercy."

Beloved, God extends His mercy through us! God extends His mercy through our prayers. As tragic as September the 11th was, God was most merciful! The next day I watched in amazement as one of the major news networks reported that there was credible evidence that the White House and Air Force One were indeed targets.

What is my perspective on all this? My understanding is that God showed me how to pray, because He wanted to release mercy. The important factor in this is not me…but God's mercy. Not, "God showed ME!," but rather, "God showed." I believe God showed similar revelation to many prayer warriors all over the world. It is not important "to whom"; what is important is that we have a God who reveals secrets. We have a God who knows everything. If we will press into Him like Daniel, with humble, broken, and repentant hearts; if we will fast and pray, I believe God will speak to us. He will reveal His counsel, and He will reveal the very prayer requests on the heart of God! That is what those two visions were! They were prayer requests on the heart of God, a heart inclined to show us mercy! He channeled this mercy through my prayer, and the prayers of thousands of others, I'm sure, who were also shown the very same thing. "Lord, teach us to pray! Lord Jesus, teach us to join in Your intercessions."

After fasting and praying according to the Word and will of God, Daniel received what he had requested. In Daniel chapter 9, he was praying for a release of mercy and the return of the Jews to their land. Ezra records that the decree that was issued in heaven was enacted on earth, as Cyrus issued the decree permitting the Jews to return to Judah and rebuild their temple. (Ezra 1:4)

WHAT DOES GOD CALL US TO DO?

Question: How do we as American Christians make sense out of what has happened, and what is happening in our world? **How do we know what it is that God is calling us to do?**

The day after the attacks, while watching the news coverage of the tremendous devastation wrought on 9/11, I asked the Lord, "What are You trying to say? What is the significance of what was hit in the attacks?"

Immediately the Holy Spirit brought to my remembrance Jeremiah 9:23-24: "Thus says the LORD: 'Let not the wise man boast in his wisdom, let not the mighty man boast in his might, nor the rich man in his riches; but let him who boasts boast in this: that he understands and knows Me, that I am the LORD who exercises lovingkindness and judgment and righteousness in all the earth.'" (NKJV)

The Holy Spirit then gave me understanding of the significance of these verses for us today. Our nation's intelligence agencies had no specific intelligence that the attacks were coming. Our *'wisdom'* failed us. The Pentagon, a symbol of our military *might*, was breached. The World Trade Center, a symbol of our *economic prosperity,* was completely destroyed. As I pondered the meaning of these verses and what we had seen the day before, a spiritual shudder went down my spiritual spine. I was frightened at the indictment of us as Christians that was contained in these verses. We do not know our God. We do not understand our God. We may know a lot about Him; but a lot of knowledge about God will fail me in this hour, and it will fail you as well. If we do not know God intimately, if we do not understand Him and His ways, then we should be frightened, because we will not know what to do. We will not have a clue as to how to respond in the days ahead.

The good news, however, is that God is calling us to seek Him anew. The good news is that any and all who seek God, and press in to know Him, will know Him. He will reveal Himself, when we seek Him with all our hearts. "You will seek me and find me when you seek me with all your heart." (Jeremiah 29:13) Beloved, let us seek the Lord with all our hearts! We really cannot afford to do anything else. What encouragement we find in Daniel 11:32: "...The people who know their God shall be strong and carry out great exploits." (NKJV) Awesome! "The people who know their God shall be strong and carry out great exploits." It is my conviction, it is my prayer, and it is my hope, that we are not living in an "Ezekiel 22:30" generation unto ultimate judgment. Rather, we are living in a "Hezekiah" generation...a generation that has the opportunity to see God relent. A generation that has the potential — if we respond to the Lord — to see mercy, revival, and restoration. That is what Hezekiah's generation experienced, and we can experience it as well.

"DO NOT BE NEGLIGENT NOW..."

Listen to these words of King Hezekiah. They are as significant for us today as they were for the Levites and the priests of his day: "Now it is in my heart to make a covenant with the LORD God of Israel, that his fierce wrath may turn from us. My sons, do not be negligent now, for the LORD has chosen you to stand before him, to serve him, and that you should minister to him and burn incense." (II Chronicles 29:10-11 NKJV)

"My sons, do not be negligent now." It is time to stand. It is time for us to stand. It is time for us to rise up. It is not time for us to sit idly or passively by, saying, "Oh well, the nation's going to hell in a handbasket; what can I do about it?" We can do a lot about it. We can do a lot about what happens in the Church in this nation, but we have got to stand up. We have been sitting for at least the last 40 years. We have got to serve the Lord and not ourselves. Are we lovers of pleasure? Are we lovers of our own lives? Or are we lovers of God? Lovers of the kingdom of God? Lovers of our neighbors and our co-workers? Lovers of the heart and the purpose of God? A God who is saying, "Serve me! Minister to me! Worship me!" We need to learn to worship the Lord, both personally and corporately, for the Lord speaks to us when we worship Him. Then we need to "burn incense." What He speaks to us, we need to offer up as incense to Him, just as I offered up those prayers for mercy for President Bush, the White House, and Air Force One. We can minister to the Lord, we can burn incense, we can join in the intercessions of Jesus.

God is calling us to be like Daniel, Ezra, and Nehemiah, who stood before Him in the era of the Persian restoration. He is calling us to be like Hezekiah, who called out to God in the face of the Assyrian threat. He is calling to us, "<u>You</u>, my Beloved, are to stand in the gap on behalf of the Church! <u>You</u> are to stand in the gap on behalf of the land. You are the ones who, through repentance and prayer, are to repair the breach and defend the city."

KINGDOM PATRIOTS

During another crossroads moment in our history, that of the Revolutionary War, it is estimated that one-third of the Colonists were Loyalists, faithful to the crown of England. They were content with the status quo. Another third, it is estimated, were indifferent. They really did not care which way the war went. One-third, a rather small minority in comparison, were patriots. Only one third.[9]

Daniel was a spiritual patriot, a "kingdom patriot." He was committed to the purposes and plans of God for his day above all else. Of course there is a difference between being an American patriot and being a kingdom patriot. Sometimes, however, I think there may be a linkage or a connection between the two. In my view, that very well may be the case in our generation. First and foremost, we must ask ourselves: to which category do we belong, as we look at our involvement in the plans of God for our generation? Are you committed to spiritual business as usual? Are you committed to "Churchianity," as usual, as it has existed in our country for the most part over the past generation? Are you indifferent? Are you so distracted, so involved in the "micro"-details of your own personal life, that the "macro"-issues of the kingdom of God and our nation really do not impact you very much?

Do you know what our greatest enemy is today as a church and as a nation? It is **apathy**. Apathy is lethal. It is a very slow death, but it is as destructive as any other enemy.

I don't know about you, but I want to be like Daniel. By God's grace, I believe I can be. Not because of who I am, but because of who God is. It does not have much to do with me; it does not have much to do with you. It has everything to do with God. We have an extraordinary God, who can take ordinary people like us and weave our prayers and our lives together with a purpose of historic proportions. That is who our God is. I want my God to be extraordinary in and through my life. I long for God's extraordinariness to be expressed in and through the Church in our day. I want to be like Daniel. I want to be a kingdom patriot.

A GRATEFUL HEART = A RESPONSIVE HEART

One variable above all else will determine which category you or I fit into — Loyalist to the status quo, indifferent bystander, or kingdom patriot. The key is to be found in how we would answer this question: **"How in touch are you with the cost of your redemption?"** How in touch am I with the cost of my redemption? That is the bottom line. How I answer that question will determine what I do with my life. As Jesus said to Simon the Pharisee in Luke 7:47, "He who has been forgiven little loves little." The corollary is true as well, "He who is forgiven much loves much." Beloved, there is not a person reading this book who has not been forgiven much! I am not talking about the "biggies," those obvious or overt sins that we may or may not have committed. I am talking about my heart, and yours — hearts that the prophet Jeremiah said are deceitful and desperately wicked. Hearts that are sinful and fleshly. It is out of that fleshliness of heart and independence of spirit that all these other sins flow.

God views my sin harshly; but God views my repentant heart mercifully. God is not easy on sin; but God is merciful and gracious to us, as repentant Christians. We have got to call a spade a spade in our own lives; otherwise, the mercy and grace of God mean very little to us. They become mere words, theological terms. Mercy: we do not get what we deserve. Grace: we get what we do not deserve. Do those words ring rich with meaning as you read them today? If you know Jesus as your personal Savior and Lord, then in God's great mercy, you have not been given what you deserve. In God's great grace, you have been granted that which you do not deserve.

Some time ago I was driving my younger son, Justin, to kindergarten. On the way, he asked me very suddenly, "Daddy, God is really very patient, isn't He?" I replied, "Yes, son, He is. He is really the most patient person." A brief pause. "Daddy, God is really merciful, isn't He?" "Yes, son, He is." Another brief pause. "Daddy, isn't it true that God the Father always had the plan to send God the Son to die for us?" "Yes, son, God the Father always had the plan to save us." Then immediately, "And Daddy, isn't it right that Jesus didn't deserve the ouchy crown and the ouchy nails? Isn't that right, Daddy? We deserved those, didn't we?"

The child shall lead the way! Could there be a more vivid picture of what Jesus did for you and me? He took my "ouchy crown," and He took yours too. He took my "ouchy" nails, and He took yours as well!

> *Were the whole realm of nature mine*
> *That were a present far too small;*
> *Love so amazing, so divine*
> *Demands my heart, my soul, my all.*[10]

Kingdom history is being written at this very hour, Beloved. May we step up to the spiritual plate. May we, like Daniel, stand in the gap.

A PRAYER IN RESPONSE
Lord Jesus, we thank You that You chose to become a man, and then to die on a cross in the finest hour of history. Thank You that in the finest hour of my life, of my personal history, when I embraced You, that You showed me mercy and grace. Thank You, Lord Jesus, that You took our "ouchy crowns," and You took our "ouchy nails." Give us spiritual enlightenment and understanding. May we truly come to know what mercy is, and what grace is. May we see the cost of our redemption. Lord, would we — would I — respond with gratitude and worship. O that we would yearn more than anything else to give You the generation that lies before us! Lord Jesus, it is all we have to give You. May we step up to the plate. May we step into the gap. Would You make us like Daniel. Would You impart to us the same spirit that You imported to him: humility, brokenness, repentance, a spirit of fasting and prayer, a heart that pleads for mercy. Lord, we want to be in the chapter of Your kingdom history that is written for this generation. We want to be kingdom patriots and spiritual patriots, Lord Jesus, because You are worthy of our complete devotion. You alone are worthy! It is in Your name we pray. Amen.

CHAPTER FOUR

Ask for the Ancient Paths

O n Sunday mornings as we drive to church, the Lewis family usually has a time of worship and prayer. On one such occasion about a month after 9/11, we listened to a powerful song about revival and awakening in our nation. When the song had finished, my then eight-year-old son, Joshua, said, *"Daddy, God is disciplining us, but God is calling us back."*

GOD'S THREE-FOLD MESSAGE TO OUR GENERATION

"Daddy, God is disciplining us, but God is calling us back." God is indeed calling us back. **What is the three-fold message of God for this generation?** I believe three themes are woven together inseparably in God's heart for us, and for this hour: **a word of hope, a call to faith, and a challenge to repentance.**

Our God is so good, so merciful, so patient. Even though we may deserve judgment in this hour, our gracious God even links His command to repent with an encouraging word of hope: a word designed to stir our faith to believe that God is not finished with us yet.

GODLY GRIEF, BUT WITH HOPE

God does call the Church of the United States of America — and the church of every nation for that matter — to repentance. He is calling us to mourn, to weep, and to fast and to pray. He calls us in brokenness and repentance to confess our sins and the sins of our fathers, that our land might be healed. God is calling us to experience what He already experiences as He looks at the state of the Church and the nation: a godly grief.

Godly grief is not a grief without hope. In fact, it is a grief imbued with much hope. Personally, over the past year, I have been more deeply grieved and burdened for America, for Israel, and for the world, than ever before in my life. I have shed more tears praying for the world in this year than in all of my life previously. Yet, at the same time, I have more faith and more hope than ever before to believe God for a powerful move of His Spirit in this day. Grief is not separated from hope, or from faith. As David tells us, "The sacrifices of God are a broken spirit; a broken and a contrite heart, O God, you will not despise." (Psalm 51:17) O Lord, would you give us such broken and contrite hearts? May we respond to the wooing and convicting of Your Spirit, that we would not miss out on what You desire to do in the generation before us.

A word of hope, a call to faith, and a command — a challenge — to repent. In chapter one, we looked at Election 2000 in light of Exodus 14, the Scripture to which God directed me on Election Day. We marveled at the miracle of mercy that God extended to our nation: the decree issued in heaven, and enacted on earth, that declared George W. Bush to be the president of the United States of America. Our great God sent us so great a mercy because He wants to instill hope. He wants to inspire faith, a faith rooted in a holy fear of God and in what He did through the election controversy and its aftermath. God moved in our nation, beloved, make no mistake about it. God sends supernatural messages through natural events. We as believers, of all people, must have ears to hear and eyes to see, or we will miss what God is saying and doing.

While granting hope and stirring faith, God calls us to repent for our prayerlessness, and to watch and to pray. Remember the words of Jesus to His disciples: "Could you men not keep watch with Me for one hour?" Jesus is still looking for people who will watch and pray; who will listen and intercede in the same spirit as Daniel.

I would like to turn our attention once more to the miracle of Election 2000 and its aftermath, for I believe future generations will regard it as one of the pivotal turning points in our history. Beloved, be of good cheer, for there is more to the story! God has not finished offering His children hope.

On December 12, 2000, George W. Bush became the president-elect of the United States of America. The next evening, during his speech from the chamber of the Texas House of Representatives, Bush called on Americans to pray — specifically for him, for the Gores, for the Congress, and for this nation. The next day the first item on President-elect Bush's schedule was a private church service — a service which he initiated. Even with all the turmoil caused by a delay of thirty-six days, George W. Bush took time to go to church and to pray.

The press was not allowed into this private service, but an on-site reporter stated that the theme of the service was the story of Moses and the Exodus. As I listened, I was stunned. The theme of the service was identical to what the Lord had laid upon my heart on Election Day**. Was this a mere coincidence? Or was God trying to tell me something?**

Was the Lord, perhaps, communicating a supernatural message through a natural event? I most certainly believe so. May we have ears to hear and eyes to see. May we know by the Spirit of God where in the Word to meditate, seek His face, and pray for this nation.

Some time later, I read the autobiography of George W. Bush, <u>A Charge to Keep</u>. The then-governor of Texas wrote about the special church service that accompanied his second gubernatorial inaugural in 1999. The pastor chose as his theme **Moses and the Exodus!** George W. Bush wrote that he was so deeply moved by what God spoke through the pastor that he was stirred to seriously consider whether God might be calling him to run for the presidency of the United States. Afterwards he asked the pastor for a copy of the message. The pastor replied that he had no notes; he had just spoken from his heart.[11] I would submit to you that he spoke from the heart of God. When the Lord spoke to me on Election Day, I had no idea what had happened on that gubernatorial inaugural day in 1999. I had no idea what the theme of the service would be after George W. Bush would be declared the president-elect. But God knew. And God, I believe, sent me that Scripture. I firmly believe this was no coincidence, but instead a confirmation that **God is speaking to the Church, and to this nation, through Exodus imagery.**

"ASK ME TO DO IT AGAIN"

Jeremiah 6:16 says, "This is what the Lord says: 'Stand at the crossroads and look; ask for the ancient paths, ask where the good way is, and walk in it, and you will find rest for your souls....'" God is calling us to look backward in order to move forward. Shortly after the resolution of the election controversy, I was sitting in my office in Israel, praying. Suddenly, it was as though the Lord began to show me a slide show, snapshot after snapshot, picturing all the events that God had used to break my heart for this nation, and for the world, in 1988 and 1989. I did not understand why the Lord was showing me these things, since I was then living in Israel. Nevertheless, I was deeply moved and began to weep. I prayed, "Lord, why are You showing me this? I don't live in the United States of America any more. What can I do about it?"

Immediately my heart began to fill with faith. The room filled with the presence of the Lord, and the Holy Spirit spoke to my heart, **"Go back and study your roots, past the Revolution, to the Pilgrims and the Puritans. Find out what they believed Me to do with this nation. <u>And ask Me to do it again</u>."**

"Ask Me to do it again."

Then I sensed the Lord saying, **"Find out what they believed concerning My purpose for Israel. There is an important future connection between the United States and Israel."** I am in deeper awe of those words as I write this than I was when the Lord first spoke them to me. Since that time, He has been answering the questions that He told me to ask. He has filled me with hope and faith for this generation in America. He has stirred me to believe that God is rallying us to His standard. He is calling us to advance His redemptive purpose — the unique, special purpose that He has for this nation — on our knees. **Will you discover the redemptive purpose for your nation and advance its fulfillment on your knees?**

Please note that I do not believe that America, alone, has a "redemptive purpose" in God's plan. I believe God has a special, unique purpose for each nation and people.

God wants to show us the answers to these questions in order to show us how to pray. Don't you want to pray the prayer requests that are on the heart of God? Scripture tells us that Jesus is continually interceding. There is not one of us that can tap into all the intercession of Jesus. Yet, if we will walk with Him and seek Him, I believe He can lead each one of us individually to share in some aspect of His intercession. He may give one believer something specific to focus on and another believer something entirely different. The intercessions of Jesus are so vast, so immense, and so awesome. By God's design we each have a part to play. In this current hour, I believe God is giving us prayer requests through the Exodus passage. **He is directing us how to pray using a certain passage as a platform, one that He offers from His Word.** When we pray God's prayer requests, in unity and in agreement, I believe that we will fill the heavenly bowls of incense in God's presence. As a result, I believe He will pour out the fulfillment of the purposes He has for the Church and for the nation in this hour.

WHAT THE PILGRIMS AND PURITANS BELIEVED ABOUT AMERICA

As I began to study about the Pilgrims and the Puritans, I discovered something that I had never known before. I learned that the Puritans were the first believing community after the Reformation to abandon a belief in what is called "Replacement Theology." Replacement Theology was a tenet of the Roman Catholic Church and the Eastern Orthodox Church. It is even the dogma of many, perhaps most, mainline Protestant denominational churches today. Replacement Theology maintains that because the Jewish people were unfaithful and rejected the Messiah, God is finished with them. None of the purposes or promises that were intended for them apply to them literally any longer. Replacement Theology asserts that all these purposes and promises are now directed instead toward the kingdom of believers. The Church is the "New Israel," according to Replacement Theology.

I am sure that many people reading this book may adhere to Replacement Theology. I respect anyone's right to believe what he sees as he reads the Scriptures. Personally, however, I am convinced that the Puritans' rejection of Replacement Theology was of great significance for the Church and Israel. Not even sixty years after the Reformation, the Puritans abandoned Replacement Theology and believed instead that God would restore Israel. By the 1570s and 1580s they were writing scholarly treatises on it. Even more importantly, they were praying for Israel's restoration, over 400 years ago! Long before 1948. Long before the birth of Zionism. Long before the re-establishment of the modern state of Israel.

At the same time, the Puritans also believed that they themselves were a people of destiny. They believed that God wanted to do something new in their day. It was their deep conviction that God was calling them, <u>like</u> the Israelites of old, to leave Europe (analogous to Egypt), to cross the Atlantic Ocean (the Red Sea), and to enter into this New World, this "Promised Land." They did *not* believe that they were replacing Israel. They did believe, however, that God's dealings with Israel were a guide for any community of people. As God had dealt with Israel, so would He deal with the nations. In their view, Israel's history was an example and guide for the nations. **The Puritans believed that if they would obey God corporately, they would see God's blessing on their community. If they disobeyed, they would see God's discipline.**

The Pilgrims and the Puritans would most definitely have agreed that "Righteousness exalts a nation, but sin is a disgrace to any people." (Proverbs 14:34) In the Puritans' view, God was planning something new, something special for the New World, and they believed God had called them to play a vital role in it, in a New Covenant sense.

REDEEMER NATION — A BEACON OF LIGHT
William Bradford, the leader of the Pilgrims for most of the

first generation in the New World, stated the reasons for the Pilgrims coming to the New World. Among them was the "great hope...for propagating and advancing the gospel of the kingdom of Christ in those remote parts of the world...though they should be but even as stepping-stones unto others for the performing of so great a work."[12] Clearly, the Pilgrims believed they had an evangelistic calling.

John Winthrop, the first governor of the Massachusetts Bay Colony, wrote <u>A Model of Christian Charity</u>, in which he laid out the vision God had given him for the colony, and for this New World. He wrote that "the New World would become a beacon of religious light," a similar theme to what Bradford had written about eight years earlier. Significantly, the seal of the Massachusetts Bay Colony bore the image of a North American Indian with the words, "Come over and help us," proceeding from his mouth. Such a choice for the official seal of the colony declared to the world that the Puritans, as their brothers in Plymouth, regarded themselves as foreign missionaries to the New World. In fact, their endeavors in North America were the first major missionary effort of English Protestantism.[13] This evangelistic theme is one thread God has sown into the history of our nation, one aspect of our redemptive purpose, as a **"redeemer nation," a beacon of religious light.**

The Puritans used that phrase, "redeemer nation." What did they mean by that? That the nation would redeem people? No, but instead that the nation would have an evangelistic purpose. That this would be a nation of great outreach to the world.

"A CITY UPON A HILL" — A MODEL OF CHRISTIAN COMMUNITY

Winthrop believed that "the New World would become a model of spiritual promise, a city upon a hill." "City upon a hill" was the very phrase that Jesus used in Matthew 5:14. In these words of Winthrop, I believe we see a second thread or aspect of the redemptive purpose God would uniquely have for this nation as a **"shining city upon a hill," a model of spiritual promise, a model of Christian charity.** The Puritan community was called to live out the New Covenant Way, loving the Lord their God with all their hearts, with all their souls, with all their minds, and with all their strength; and loving their neighbor as themselves.

A PROMISED LAND — A REFUGE FROM RELIGIOUS PERSECUTION

A third aspect of God's redemptive purpose for the United States is reflected in the testimony of William Penn, the founder of Pennsylvania. Penn was an avowed atheist. He converted to Christianity at the age of twenty-two and became a powerful preacher of the Gospel. He was imprisoned in England three times for his faith. While imprisoned in the Tower of London, William Penn dreamed and prayed that God would grant him an opportunity to found a colony in the New World, one characterized by religious freedom. It would be a refuge for persecuted believers, but also a Christian commonwealth, demonstrating liberty, justice, and peace.

William Penn did come to the New World in 1682. He established the colony of Pennsylvania with its capital in Philadelphia, the "city of brotherly love." Interestingly enough, Philadelphia would later become the second capital of our nation. The significance of this is not lost upon us. The "city of brotherly love" was yet one more picture of the calling of this New World to be characterized by the New Covenant Way: love for God and love for one another.

Most significantly, Penn granted all religious groups complete freedom of worship in Pennsylvania. His colony became a haven for all who were fleeing religious persecution. As such, Pennsylvania exemplified what I believe to be the third aspect of God's redemptive purpose for America. America would indeed, as a bastion of liberty, be seen by the poor and oppressed as a "Promised Land."

Penn's personal Bible has survived to this day. **Would you hazard a guess as to what the most underlined portion of his Bible is? The book of Exodus!** He was yet one more "founding grandfather" who, like the Puritans before him, likened the removal of persecuted Christians from Europe to the Exodus of the Israelites from Egypt. He too saw the Exodus imagery in the discovery and settlement of the New World.

DESTINED TO BLESS THE JEWISH PEOPLE

Lastly, another expression of God's redemptive purpose for America is found in seed form in the belief which God sowed into the hearts of our Puritan forebears concerning **the restoration of Israel, both physically and spiritually.** They were praying and longing for such a restoration 400 years ago. They blessed Israel and the Jewish people through their beliefs, unique for that era, and through their prayers. I believe God desires to breathe on those prayers in our day, so that our nation would arise and bless Israel and the Jewish people. This significant theme will be the subject of later chapters in this book.

I have outlined what I believe are four aspects of the redemptive purpose God has for our nation: a "redeemer nation" (evangelism), "a shining city upon a hill" (a model of New Covenant community), a "promised land" (refuge from religious persecution), and a blessing to Israel. **A "redeemer nation"; "a shining city on a hill," a "promised land," and a blessing to Israel.** I would submit to you that the seeds which God sowed into our national consciousness in Plymouth and in Massachusetts Bay are some of the most significant, if not the most significant, **righteous roots of our nation.** It is my earnest prayer and fervent hope that these righteous roots will once again bear fruit in our generation.

"DO IT AGAIN"

God is calling us to return to our roots. What God did once, He can do again. What God spoke to our founding grandfathers, could He not speak to us? Did He mean it when He spoke then, but not four hundred years later? Beloved, God is breathing on the Exodus account, partially to point us to our "exodus," the exodus of our founding grandfathers from Europe to this New World. May we rise up and pray for the mighty fulfillment of God's redemptive purpose for our nation. Cry out to Him in your prayer closets, in your car, in your coming and going. **"O God! Do it again!** Make us a lighthouse for the Gospel, a model of Christian charity, a place of refuge, and a blessing to Israel. Grant that we might fulfill these purposes in our generation."

I have heard that by the time of the American Revolution,

approximately 75% of the American colonists were of Puritan descent. How incredibly significant that at the time of our Revolution, 75% of the population would be of Puritan descent. This fact underscores the importance and impact of our Puritan heritage. Surely their godly influence is a chief reason for so much of the blessing with which God has graced this nation. Surely this history of the Pilgrims and the Puritans is the most significant righteous root of our nation. **It is this root that I long to see bear fruit in a fresh expression of God's redemptive purpose for our nation.**

THE "AMERICAN EXODUS"

As I continued to study the spiritual roots of our country, I was amazed by the profound national identification with the Old and New Testaments in the soul and spirit of the American people. The Lord gripped me with these words from a December 27, 1982 *Newsweek* article, "How the Bible Made America":

> Historians are now discovering that the Bible, perhaps even more than the Constitution, is our founding document: the source of [the belief] in **the United States as a special, sacred nation, a people called by God to establish a model society, a beacon to the world....**Only one other nation has ever looked to the Bible to find a warrant for its very existence: Israel, whose early history is actually written in it. The foundation of this [belief] was laid by the New England Puritans who literally 'discovered America' in the Bible.[14] [Emphasis added]

Seeing the birth of the United States as a new expression of the story of ancient Israel became a major theme in Colonial America. During the Continental Congress in 1776, Benjamin Franklin proposed that the seal of the United States of America picture the image of Moses, leading the Israelites across the Red Sea. Franklin's proposal was not ultimately adopted; nevertheless, it is very significant for us, as we look at history, to find clues concerning the purpose God is weaving into the history of our nation.[15]

Similarly, Thomas Jefferson proposed that the seal of the new nation bear the image of Israel, led through the wilderness by the Biblical pillar of cloud and pillar of fire.[16] Though not known for his spiritual orthodoxy, Thomas Jefferson said in his second inaugural address, "I shall need, too, the favor of that Being in whose hands we are, who led our forefathers as Israel of old" [like Israel of old, as Israel of old, similarly to Israel of old] "from their native land and planted them in a country flowing with all the necessities and comforts of life." [17] [Emphasis added]

Late one afternoon, just moments after reading about Franklin and Jefferson's proposals, my younger son Justin came into my office and asked me to go outside and ride bikes with him. I took him outside, and as we turned down the street, I looked up into the sky and saw a huge, gray, pillar-shaped cloud. Shining out from the cloud on all sides was the most brilliant, fiery light. I paused, bowed my head, and prayed, "Lord, be a pillar of cloud by day and a pillar of fire by night for our family! We want to go where You're going. We want Your Presence to go with us." It was just a simple, heartfelt prayer, and then suddenly, the Holy Spirit arrested me in my tracks. "Do you not understand what I have shown you? Do you not understand why I have shown you these facts about the proposed seal? Why I brought you outside to show you this cloud? **I gave you Exodus 14 not just for the election, but for the nation itself, in this period of history. This is a moment of destiny for America.** The nation is at a crossroads. I am calling this nation to a new beginning, just as I did Israel at the time of the Exodus. **I'm calling my Body in America to return to its roots."**

"ROLL AWAY THE REPROACH"

When God chose to reveal Himself to Moses, how did He do so? Of course, we all know the answer to that question: a burning bush. What the Lord has spoken to my heart is that Election 2000 and its miraculous resolution was intended to be a sign, a "burning bush" revelation to our nation. Through the election of George W. Bush, we witnessed a burning "bush": a glorious manifestation of God's presence, power, mercy, and grace upon our nation. What is the Lord saying? He is speaking to us, as He spoke to Moses and that generation of Israelites. He is calling us "out of Egypt," out of the "fleshpots of Egypt." [KJV] What is God saying to us as the body of Christ? "Forsake Egypt! Forsake Egypt and all that it stands for!" The flesh...the world...its influence...the dominion of the enemy in our lives. What that means specifically may be something very different for each one of us, but the Lord has the power to speak about what is left of Egypt in my life, and what is left of Egypt in your life.

After the Israelites crossed the Jordan River, the first item of business was to circumcise all the males born during the wilderness years. No one had been circumcised in the wilderness. Scripture says the Israelites named the place "Gilgal," because "God rolled away the reproach" of Egypt. (Joshua 5:9) It was a new beginning, a fresh start for that generation. Likewise, God wants to roll away the reproach of Egypt in my life. He wants to roll away the reproach of Egypt in your life. He wants to roll away the reproach of Egypt from the Church, so that we as believers may rise up and enter into the land, that is, into the purposes of God for us in this hour.

It is time for us to enter the heart of God, to enter His destiny for us. It is time to ask Him to move us as a Church, and to move us as a nation, like a pillar of cloud by day and a pillar of fire by night. Our God is the same yesterday, today, and forever. As He called to the Israelites then, so He calls to us now. Psalm 42:7 proclaims, *"Deep calls to deep!"* I am not sure as to the complete meaning of this verse. Yet, surely part of it is that something deep in the heart of God calls to something deep in the heart of man. Do you hear Him? Do you hear the Lord? From the election, its resolution; even through September the 11th — **do you hear the voice of God?** A deep call and a deep cry from the heart of God Himself, calling unto the deep of our spirits, that we would respond, "Yes, Lord, we hear you! Yes, Lord, we see! We want to hear! We want to see! We want to understand! We want to discern! We want to repent! We want to lay down all that remains of 'Egypt' in our lives. Roll away the reproach from us! Fulfill your purpose for me, for my spouse, for my family, for my church, for the Church, and for this nation."

"Stand in the crossroads and look; ask for the ancient paths. Ask where the good way is, and walk in it," beloved, and we will find rest. We will find deliverance. We will find — in a way we never have before — our God! Blessed be His name!

A PRAYER IN RESPONSE

Father in Heaven, thank You that You speak to Your people. That You speak to us in every era and in every generation. Thank you for how You spoke to Moses and to the Israelites. Thank You that in some way, in the mystery of Your sovereignty and Your divine purposes, You choose to speak to the Church and the nation through the imagery of the Exodus again. Father, may we not be dull of hearing — give us ears to hear. May we not be blind of sight — give us eyes to see. Give us hearts that receive Your revelation in the fear of the Lord! Give us spirits that respond in repentance. Even though we may have personally left Egypt when we embraced Jesus, there is still much of Egypt left in us. We have left Egypt, but it has not left us. O Father, forgive me, and forgive us! Show us where we are still captivated by the "fleshpots of Egypt." Show us, uniquely, the sin in our hearts and lives that You want us to repent of. Roll away the reproach, we ask You. We want to confess our sins. We want to repent. We want to turn from sin to You. We want You to lead us supernaturally, radically, powerfully, in and through Your Church, to impact America in a nationally-transforming awakening. Lord, we pray You would do it for the sake of the remnant that is praying at this hour. May it increase. We pray You would do it for the sake of the remnant that has prayed in every generation. We pray You would do it for the sake of the Pilgrims and the Puritans, who came to this land out of a godly motivation which You planted in their hearts. Breathe on the prayers they prayed 400 years ago. Father, breathe on them again! Do again what You did in their generation. Ultimately, Lord God, we pray that You would do it for Jesus' sake, for He is worthy, as are You, our Blessed Father. O, may we love You and adore You! May everything else in our lives spring from a worshipful spirit, penetrated by Your truth. In the name of Jesus Christ, our Savior and Lord, Amen.

CHAPTER FIVE

Revival as in the Days of Hezekiah

I n this chapter let us continue our search for the "ancient paths." (Jeremiah 6:16) So far, our study of the Exodus account and our early history has proven most fruitful. We have examined not only the literal Exodus, but also our American "Exodus" and the significance of the Puritan legacy for us today. We have discovered that **God has a powerful message for the generation before us. The message: as America stands at the crossroads, God calls us back to our roots.**

As we look back to our "Exodus" generation, is there perhaps a generation similar to ours that is described in Scripture? Does our generation have a Biblical equivalent, that is, a generation that the Lord also called to harken back to its roots? Even to the Exodus specifically? Could such a generation be instructive for us as we look to our future? I believe the answer is "yes." That Biblically equivalent generation will be the primary focus of this chapter.

Before I describe it, however, let me share a further word of personal testimony by way of background.

On New Year's Eve 2000, I attended a prayer vigil at a Messianic congregation atop Mt. Carmel in Haifa, Israel. The prayer focus was revival for the land of Israel — for both the Jews and the Arabs. As I joined in praying for that country that I love so much, I was praying simultaneously for our own nation — for revival and spiritual awakening in the United States of America.

Throughout the evening, the Lord kept bringing to my mind **Psalm 85:6: "Will you not revive us again, that your people may rejoice in you?"** I opened my Bible to Psalm 85 and began to read. I noticed that the Psalm was divided into three parts. In the first part, the Psalmist remembers how God has restored his people in the past. How God has been favorable to the land, forgiven iniquity, brought back from captivity, and covered sin. (vs. 1-3)

Then in verse 4, there is a shift to a current, contemporary appeal. "Restore us again, O God our Savior, and put away your displeasure toward us. Will you be angry with us forever? Will you prolong your anger through all generations? Will you not revive us again, that your people may rejoice in you? Show us your unfailing love, O LORD, and grant us your salvation." (vs. 4-7) In verse eight, the Psalmist turns to God's future response to his appeal: "I will listen to what God the LORD will say; he promises peace to his people, his saints — but let them not return to folly. Surely his salvation is near those who fear him, that his glory may dwell in our land." (vs. 8-9)

All evening the Holy Spirit kept quickening this Psalm in my spirit, particularly verse 6: "Will you not revive us again, that your people may rejoice in you?" I approached the pastor who was leading the prayer meeting, and shared the Psalm with him. Just before midnight he called me forward to pray the Psalm over the nation. I shared briefly about the psalm and then literally prayed the psalm before the Lord. The worship team began a closing set of worship, and I walked back to my seat. As I began to worship, once again the Lord spoke to my heart in a way that was so clear and powerful, like a lightning bolt: **"I'm ready to answer your question."** I was so taken by surprise, I didn't know what question the Lord meant! Sometimes that's the way it is when the Lord speaks to our hearts. It does not come out of us! It surprises us. I responded, "What question?" The Lord replied, "The question you've been asking all night: 'Will you not revive us again that your people may rejoice again in you?' *I am ready to answer your question. I* *am ready to revive America again. I greatly desire to do this. But the Church must respond to Me. The Church must seek me in the spirit of Hezekiah."*

"IN THE SPIRIT OF HEZEKIAH"

I immediately opened up the Bible I had with me. I had grabbed it while hurrying out the door that evening. It was my sister's pocket Bible. How I ended up with my sister's pocket Bible in Israel, I do not know. Anyway, I turned to **the story of King Hezekiah in II Chronicles 29-32** and began to glance at these chapters. I noticed certain verses had been underlined — when, or by whom, I had no clue. But as I read them, I was spellbound, because each underlined word seemed to have been underscored that evening by the Holy Spirit Himself. It was as though He was highlighting key aspects of the Hezekiah revival, and what He had done to move so radically and powerfully in that generation.

Let us first explore these underlined verses and highlight their significance for us today. Then I will pick up the story where I left off.

Hezekiah was twenty-five years old when he became king, and he reigned in Jerusalem twenty-nine years. His mother's name was Abijah daughter of Zechariah. He did what was right in the eyes of the LORD, just as his father David had done. In the first month of the first year of his reign, he opened the doors of the house of the LORD and repaired them. He brought in the priests and the Levites, assembled them in the square on the east side, and said: 'Listen to me, Levites! Consecrate yourselves now and consecrate the temple of the LORD, the God of your fathers. Remove all defilement from the sanctuary. Our fathers were unfaithful; they did evil in the eyes of the LORD our God and forsook him. They turned their faces away from the Lord's dwelling place and turned their backs on him....They did not burn incense or present any burnt offerings....Therefore, the anger of the LORD has fallen on Judah and Jerusalem; he has made them an object of dread and horror and scorn, as you can see with your own eyes....Now I intend to make a covenant with the LORD, the God of Israel, so that his fierce anger will turn away from us. My sons, do not be negligent now, for the LORD has chosen you to stand before him and serve him, to minister before him and burn incense.' (II Chronicles 29:1-8, 10-11)

CLEANSE THE TEMPLE

What is the first thing that Hezekiah did? He opened the doors of the temple and repaired them. He called the Levites to purify themselves, and to consecrate themselves to the Lord. That is also God's message for the Church today. **He is saying it is time to clean house, just like Hezekiah did.** Time to open the doors of the temple, both individually in our lives, and corporately in our local churches. We need to open up the doors and ask the Lord to cleanse us. Every defilement and abomination that impede a revelation of the glory of God must go!

One Sunday after church, my older son Joshua asked me for three envelopes. I gave him the three envelopes, a little curious as to what they were for. A few minutes later he approached me again, "Daddy, I have some money in these three envelopes, and I want to write some words on them. Would you help me spell them right? I know how to write 'The Poor,' and 'The Church,' but I don't know how to spell 'Missionary.'"

After I spelled it for him, Joshua said, "Daddy, I put money into these three envelopes because today at church we talked about how our lives are the temple and that we don't want idols in the temple. We want to worship God. And you know, Daddy, **an idol can be anything that's more important to me than God!**" He then added, "I felt like God was telling me that money is too important to me. So I want to take some of my money and I want to give it to the church, and to the missionaries, and to the poor next Sunday."

The Lord so often speaks to me through my children in moments like these, when I know He is penetrating their hearts — and mine. The Lord desires that we open up our hearts, asking Him, "What are the idols in my life? What are my idolatries? What are my treasures?" Jesus said, "Do not store up for yourselves treasure on earth, where moth and rust destroy, and where thieves break in and steal. But store up for yourselves treasures in heaven, where moth and rust do not destroy, and where thieves do not break in and steal. For where your treasure is, there your heart will be also." (Matthew 6:19-20)

Where is your treasure? Is it a heavenly treasure? Or an earthly treasure?

RENEW THE COVENANT

After cleansing the temple, Hezekiah made a covenant with the Lord. (vs. 10-11) The Lord called Hezekiah's generation not only to repent, but also to renew their covenant with Him. In the same way, God calls us not only to repent, but to **return to our righteous roots,** renewing a covenantal relationship with Him. God calls us to stand before Him and serve Him, to minister and to burn incense, just as our founding grandfathers did some 400 years ago.

The covenant the Pilgrims made with the Lord is still instructive for us today. Here is an excerpt from the Mayflower Compact, written before the Pilgrims landed at Plymouth:

In the name of God, Amen. We whose names are underwritten, the loyal subjects of our dread sovereign Lord King James by the Grace of God of Great Britain, France, Ireland, King, Defender of the faith, etc.

Having undertaken, for the glory of God and advancement of the Christian Faith, and Honour of our King and Country, a Voyage to plant the First Colony in the Northern Parts of Virginia, do by these presents solemnly and mutually in the presence of God and of one another, Covenant and Combine ourselves together into a Civil Body Politic, for our better ordering and preservation, and furtherance of the ends aforesaid; [What were the "ends aforesaid?" The glory of God and the advancement of the Christian faith.] and by virtue hereof to enact, constitute and frame such just and equal Laws, Ordinances, Acts,

Constitutions and Offices, from time to time, as shall be thought most meet and convenient for the general good of the Colony, unto which we promise all due submission and obedience. In witness whereof we have hereunder inscribed our names at Cape Cod, the 11ᵗʰ of November, in the year of the reign of our Sovereign Lord King James, of England, France and Ireland the eighteenth, and of Scotland the fifty-fourth. A*nno Domini* 1620.[18]

Ten years later the Puritans arrived in Massachusetts under the leadership of John Winthrop. While still aboard the *Arbella*, Winthrop preached a sermon entitled <u>A Model of Christian Charity</u>. Note his emphasis on our commission and our covenant:

This love among Christians is a real thing, not imaginary…as absolutely necessary to the [well]being of the body of Christ, as the sinews and other ligaments of a natural body are to the [well]being of that body….We are a company, professing ourselves fellow members of Christ, [and thus] we ought to account ourselves knit together by this bond of love….Thus stands the cause between God and us: we are entered into covenant with Him for this work. We have taken out a Commission; the Lord has given us leave to draw our own articles….If the Lord shall please to hear us, and bring us in peace to the place we desire, then hath He ratified this Covenant and sealed our Commission, [and] will expect a strict performance of the Articles contained in it. But if we shall neglect the observance of these Articles…the Lord will surely break out in wrath against us.

Now the only way to avoid this shipwreck and to provide for our posterity, is to follow the counsel of Micah, to do justly, to love mercy, to walk humbly with our God. For this end, we must be knit together in this work as one man….We must hold a familiar commerce together in all meekness, gentleness, patience, and liberality. We must delight in each other, make one another's condition our own, rejoice together, mourn together, labor and suffer together, always having before our eyes our Commission and Community…as members of the same body. So shall we keep the unity of the Spirit in the bond of peace….We shall find that the God of Israel is among us, when ten of us shall be able to resist a thousand of our enemies, when He shall make us a praise and glory, that men of succeeding plantations shall say, 'The Lord make it like that of New England.' For we must consider that we shall be as a City upon a Hill.[19]

What a legacy! The impact of these two covenants on the New World cannot be overestimated. They are both examples of the righteous roots of our nation. God is calling us back to this kind of covenantal commitment.

A couple of generations later, when the colony became prosperous, the Pilgrims' and Puritans' descendants became apathetic and materialistic. **"Religion begat prosperity, and the daughter devoured the mother,"** as Puritan scholar Cotton Mather expressed it.[20] He could just as easily have been speaking of us today. We live in a very materialistic generation in this nation, and in the Western world. God is calling us back to the spirit of these covenants written into the spiritual fabric of our nation 400 years ago.

The perspective of the Puritans is clearly evident in this description of the first church that they founded:

Although the number of the faithful people of Christ are but few, yet their longing desire to gather into a church was very great…Having fasted and prayed with humble acknowledgement of their own unworthiness to be called of Christ to do so worthy a work, they joined together in a holy Covenant with the Lord and with one another, promising by the Lord's assistance to walk together in exhorting, admonishing and rebuking one another, and to cleave to the Lord with a full purpose of heart….[21]

A holy fear of the Lord and undivided hearts characterized the Puritans and the Pilgrims. **They understood that God had called them as believers into a covenantal relationship with Him, as they charted a new course in a new land.** Hezekiah shared this understanding in his day. God wants us to do the same thing personally, and as families and churches: **renew our covenant with God.** I believe it is important that we renew these covenants from which I quoted above. I encourage you to read them. I encourage you to pray over them with your families. Pray that the Church of this nation would renew its covenant with the Lord.

GATHER THE ELDERS

The next item on Hezekiah's agenda was to gather the civil leaders, the elders at the gate. "Early the next morning King Hezekiah gathered the city officials together and went up to the temple of the LORD." (29:20) We must do the same in every city in this nation. I encourage you to pray that God would rally pastors and para-church leaders, the spiritual gatekeepers of our cities, as well as believing civil leaders, to **pray together in unity for revival and spiritual awakening.** In many cities all over this nation pastors have been gathering, by the hundreds even, to pray once a year for three or four days — simply to seek the face of God. Many also meet on a weekly or monthly basis to pray for their cities. I believe God is saying that it's time for the spiritual leadership of our cities to come together in unity and prayer, beseeching the Lord for revival and awakening. Pray that a holy fear of the Lord would fall on our pastors and our civil leaders as well. O, that they would be so gripped by the fate of our nation as it hangs in the balance, that they would consider unified prayer among the greatest works that they could do! We must lay aside all denominationalism. As Augustine said, "Unity on the essentials, liberty on the non-essentials, and in everything love." Our labels as Methodists, Baptists, Lutherans, Episcopalians, Presbyterians, Evangelicals, and Charismatics are secondary to our calling as Christians to rally together **in unity and prayer to ask God to revive the Church, and to pour out awakening on our land.**

CALL THE NATION

After rallying the spiritual and civil leaders, Hezekiah then called the nation to repent and return to its roots.

> Hezekiah sent word to all Israel and Judah and also wrote letters to Ephraim and Manasseh, inviting them to come to the temple of the Lord in Jerusalem and celebrate the Passover to the LORD, the God of Israel....They decided to send a proclamation throughout Israel, from Beersheba to Dan, calling the people to come to Jerusalem and cele-brate the Passover to the LORD, the God of Israel....The couriers went from town to town in Ephraim and Manasseh, as far as Zebulun, but the people scorned and ridiculed them. Nevertheless, some men of Asher, Manasseh and Zebulun humbled themselves and went to Jerusalem. Also in Judah the hand of God was on the people to give them unity of mind to carry out what the king and his officials had ordered, following the word of the LORD. (II Chronicles 30:1, 5, 10-12)

According to the Chronicles account, it was the "word of the Lord" that called the people of Judah to celebrate the Passover and return to their roots. Likewise, I believe it is the word of the Lord that calls us to do the same in our generation. In response to Hezekiah's proclamation, the people of Judah and a large remnant from several northern tribes gathered in Jerusalem to celebrate the Passover. And what a celebration it was! They celebrated for seven days, then decided to continue the celebration for seven more days. "There was great joy in Jerusalem, for since the days of Solomon son of David king of Israel there had been nothing like this in Jerusalem. The priests and Levites stood to bless the people, and God heard them, for their prayer reached heaven, his holy dwelling place." (II Chronicles 30:26-27)

What a beautiful picture of renewal! The Lord visited His people in a way unparalleled since the days of Solomon. **I believe our Heavenly Father will move in the same way again if we will seek Him as did Hezekiah and his generation. He will revive us,**

renew us, and awaken our land. II Chronicles 31:1 describes the fruit of this revival:

> When all this had ended, the Israelites who were there went out to the towns of Judah, smashed the sacred stones and cut down the Asherah poles. They destroyed the high places and the altars throughout Judah and Benjamin and in Ephraim and Manasseh. After they had destroyed all of them, the Israelites returned to their own towns and to their own property.

This revived remnant destroyed **all the idols, all the high places, all the images...they destroyed them all.** That's a pretty far-reaching revival! Hezekiah's generation experienced not only a revival, but **a nationally-transforming awakening.**

A CONFIRMING SIGN

Now let's return to New Year's Eve 2000 and the rest of the story. As I finished reading these Scriptures, I prayed, "Lord, I believe this is Your heart for our nation." The Lord then gave me an opportunity to proclaim these verses in prayer. As I did so, the New Year 2001 dawned. I believe that even this timing was significant. It was as though God was saying, "I've given you an expression of My heart's desire for this new year, for this new decade, as you move into this new century."

I drove home early that morning of January 1, 2001, praying, "Lord, I believe You have spoken to my heart; but confirm it. Show me that indeed this is You."

Two mornings later, while I was meditating and praying over these passages, the Lord filled my heart with faith and hope. I looked up to heaven, and prayed, "Lord, would you please send me a sign! Would you please send me an external confirmation that this is the word of the Lord?"

As I closed my prayer and glanced across the room, I noticed a children's coloring book lying on the couch in the living room. An intercessor friend of ours had mailed it to us as a Christmas gift for my sons. My older son, Joshua, had apparently been reading it before school and had left it on the couch. The coloring book was opened to the front page. On it were two words in big, bold black letters, horizontally and vertically across the page, like this:

H E Z E K I A H
E
Z
E
K
I
A
H

I was completely overwhelmed. I don't know about you, but **I have never seen a "Hezekiah" coloring book in my life.** I have seen children's coloring books about Noah, Joseph, Moses, David, and Daniel, but never about Hezekiah.[22] I picked up the coloring book and began to look through it. Amazingly enough, the first few pages corresponded almost exactly to some of the Scriptures that had been underlined in my Bible!

Our God speaks in many ways. He speaks through children. He can even speak through children's coloring books! Our God graciously speaks to offer us hope, to call us to faith, and to move us to repent.

CONFIRMATION FROM HISTORY

Shortly thereafter, the Lord led me to a sermon written by Solomon Stoddard, the grandfather of Jonathan Edwards. Most Christians are familiar with Jonathan Edwards, known as the "Father of the Great Awakening." But, most of us have probably never heard of Solomon Stoddard. It was actually Solomon Stoddard who sowed the seeds for the Great Awakening, witnessing what he called five "mini-harvests" during his ministry. When he became too old to handle all the pastoral responsibilities of the Northampton Church, his grandson came to help him. After Stoddard died, Jonathan Edwards became the pastor. A great revival then broke out in 1734 under Edwards' leadership.

Solomon Stoddard's sermon from 1712 was entitled "On the Outpouring of the Spirit of God." [23] In one paragraph, he wrote that the length of revival depends entirely upon the Lord: "This reviving is sometimes of longer, and sometimes of shorter Continuance. Sometimes Religion flourishes in a Country for a great many years together. So it did for twenty-nine Years **in the days of Hezekiah,** 2 Chronicles 29:1...." In the very next paragraph he described the posture of God's people, praying for revival. God has to send revival; we cannot. We are not the ones who initiate it. Stoddard wrote, "God is very Arbitrary [unpredictable] in this Matter. The People of God are praying, and waiting for this Mercy. **Psalm 85:6 — 'Wilt Thou not revive us again, that Thy people may rejoice in Thee.' "** [Emphasis added]

OUR "HEZEKIAH GENERATION"

I was absolutely stunned as I read these two paragraphs. In two back-to-back paragraphs of one sermon from the grandfather of the spiritual awakenings in our nation, were the very two passages the Lord had given me on New Year's Eve: II Chronicles 29 (the Hezekiah revival) and Psalm 85:6. **What was God saying to me then? What is God saying to us now? I truly believe God is saying that we are living in a Hezekiah generation!** As Israel and Judah strayed from the Lord, so has the United States departed from His commands and precepts. Yet as the Lord beckoned to Hezekiah's generation, so He beckons to ours. God called the people of Judah to "clean house," consecrate themselves, and renew their covenant with Him. God calls us to do the same. God had mercy on a repentant Judah and moved powerfully to revive them. I believe with all my heart that God desires to move just as powerfully in our day.

The prophet Micah warned Hezekiah's generation that if they did not repent, judgment would fall. Jeremiah records:

Micah of Moresheth prophesied in the days of Hezekiah king of Judah, and spoke to all the people of Judah, saying, 'Thus says the Lord of hosts: "Zion shall be plowed like a field, Jerusalem shall become heaps of ruins; and the mountain of the temple like the bare hills of the forest." ' (Jeremiah 26:18)

What was Hezekiah's response to this prophetic word of judgment?

> Did Hezekiah and all Judah ever put him to death? Did he not fear the Lord and seek the LORD's favor? **And the LORD relented** concerning the doom which he had pronounced against them.... (Jeremiah 26:19) [Emphasis added]

Hezekiah feared the Lord and sought His favor, and the Lord relented! He did not send judgment; instead He sent, arguably, the greatest revival in the history of the kingdoms of Israel and Judah.

That, I believe, is what God desires to do for us. **We are potentially a "Hezekiah generation," and God is calling us to look back to our roots.** Just as the celebration of the Passover was the centerpiece of that great Biblical revival, so God is calling us to look back to our roots, to our American "Exodus," to the righteous foundation laid by the Pilgrims and the Puritans. God desires to reconnect us with our historical and our Biblical roots, awakening in us a renewed faith in, and commitment to, our destiny in God. God desires that the Church of this great nation, and this nation itself, be once more be a "redeemer nation," a beacon of Christian truth; a "shining city upon a hill," a model of Christian charity and spiritual promise; a "promised land," a haven and refuge for persecuted peoples; and, fourthly, a blessing to Israel.

Could it be that our generation will see revival, as in the days of Hezekiah? Could it be that the Fourth Great Awakening — one that, I hope, will be the greatest in our history — might lie ahead of us? Dare we hope? Dare we believe, and take these passages and this history as prayer requests to our God? I dare say, "Yes!" Do we have the courage to repent? To take a searching and fearless moral inventory in the presence of our God? Beloved, we must clean house. **We must "get the rubbish out."** We must consecrate ourselves to the Lord. This is a day of consecration, and we must renew our covenantal relationship with the Lord. God is commanding us to repent! Do we fully grasp that? God is commanding the Church in this country to repent!

I believe that as we repent, He calls to pray two requests, each an expression of the New Covenant Way to which we are called. "Lord, teach me first and foremost to love You the way I was created to love You, with all my heart, with all my soul, with all my mind, and with all my strength! And secondly, teach me to love others as Jesus would love them, and to bless them in His name." If we would pray those two things, can you imagine the spiritual passion that would ignite our hearts? The love of Jesus that would swell our breast and overflow into the lives of others!

"My people must seek me in the spirit of Hezekiah."

A PRAYER IN RESPONSE

Heavenly Father, grant that we might seek You in the spirit of Hezekiah. Grant that we might seek You with the same spirit that our Pilgrim and Puritan forebears sought You. Grant that we would desire more than anything else to treasure You, and to walk according to the New Covenant way: to love You with all our heart, soul, mind, and strength, and to love our neighbor as ourselves. O, Father, we pray that in Your great mercy You would teach us to repent. Grant us repentance in Your presence, and grant it often, that we might know the beauty of the gospel, and the freshness of Your mercies which are new every morning. Lord, teach us to love You the way we were created to love You, for we were built for nothing less. Teach us to love others as Jesus would love them. Merciful Father, would You honor these steps of obedience and indeed revive us again, that we might rejoice in You. For Jesus' sake, we pray, that our people and the peoples of the earth would know that He is God. Amen.

CHAPTER SIX

George W. Bush:
A Charge to Keep

The Lord was not yet finished speaking to me that morning of January 3, 2001. After confirming His heart's desire to revive us as in the days of Hezekiah, the Lord led me to the parallel passage in II Kings 18. I turned to it and began to read:

> In the 3rd year of Hoshea son of Elah king of Israel, Hezekiah son of Ahaz king of Judah began to reign. He was twenty-five years old when he became king, and he reigned in Jerusalem twenty-nine years. His mother's name was Abijah daughter of Zechariah. He did what was right in the eyes of the LORD, just as his father David had done. He removed the high places, smashed the sacred stones and cut down the Asherah poles....Hezekiah trusted in the LORD, the God of Israel. There was no one like him among all the kings of Judah, either before him or after him. He held fast to the LORD and did not cease to follow him; he the kept commands the LORD had given Moses. And the LORD was with him; he was successful in whatever he undertook. (II Kings 18:1-3, 4a, 5-7a)

Notice that in this passage, we are told that Hezekiah's father was Ahaz, the most wicked king Judah had known to that point in her history. He was the first king of Judah to sacrifice his sons in the fire. (II Chronicles 28:3) He engaged in unprecedented wickedness. Who would have thought during the reign of Ahaz that revival could be just around the corner? Who would have thought that Hezekiah, having had such a godless father, could be used to bring revival to the nation?

Note as well, however, that this passage also tells us that Hezekiah's mother's name was Abi [Abijah], which means "God my father." His maternal grandfather's name was Zechariah, "the LORD remembers." The Lord tells us these names for a reason. I believe it was through the influence of his mother and his maternal grandfather that a seed was sown in his life, a seed that later bore much fruit through his godly leadership during the revival. Similarly, we have been living in an era of unprecedented wickedness in our nation. Yet the Lord, I believe, desires to visit us — if we will seek Him as Hezekiah did. We must not be discouraged by the darkness that we have seen and that we currently witness, because the Lord can cause a light to shine very brightly in the darkness.

PRESIDENT BUSH'S 'HEZEKIAH' CALLING

As I read the above passage, the Lord deeply touched me. The Holy Spirit spoke to my heart, **"George W. Bush has a 'Hezekiah calling' for the United States of America, but he doesn't know it yet. He knows he has some kind of calling. He believes he has a charge to keep, but he doesn't know what the full nature of his calling is. I want you to pray that George W. Bush receives a full revelation of the calling I have on his life, and that he would enter into that in the fear of the Lord."**

As I sat before the Lord pondering these words, the Holy Spirit spoke to me again, "I have another sign for you that this is an expression of my heart. **Lynn is going to become pregnant, and you will have a girl, and you will name her Abby, after Hezekiah's mother.**"

That month, Lynn became pregnant, and nine months later on October the 16ᵗʰ, 2001, Abigail — "Abby" — Diane Lewis was born.

On Inauguration Day, January 20, 2001, George W. Bush made a very significant proclamation. He declared that his first full day in office would be a day of national prayer and thanksgiving. On the first day of the first month of his first year in office, our new president called us to prayer. Compare that with what Hezekiah did: "In the first month of the first year of his reign, he [Hezekiah] opened the doors of the temple of the LORD and repaired them." (II Chronicles 29:3) Is there a parallel between Hezekiah and George Bush?

I should add at this point that I do not believe all of this is limited to George W. Bush alone. First of all, he certainly cannot govern for a generation as Hezekiah did. It is my hope, however, that we might have a series of leaders with the heart of Hezekiah that would follow George W. Bush. Secondly, in our democratic form of government, power does not reside in the hands of one man, but is rather divided between the three branches of our government. I believe God is calling many civil "elders" in the executive, legislative, and judicial branches of our government to walk before God as Hezekiah did. Before his death, Bill Bright, the founder and first president of Campus Crusade for Christ, said that a larger number of godly officials serve in our national government now than at any time over the past fifty years. Surely, God has raised up these men and women for such a time as this!

Please do not misunderstand me. I am not suggesting that George Bush fully understood the significance of this first national prayer proclamation. I do believe, however, that what he did as a sincere man, seeking God, was a sign or a message to the Church. God, through George W. Bush's proclamation, was speaking to us, calling the Church to prayer and calling us to clean out the temple. O, that we would have hearing ears and responsive hearts.

A week later, on Super Bowl Sunday, George Bush was asked, "If you could give one message to all of the people who are watching all over the world, what would it be?" George W. Bush uttered three simple, yet profound words: "Love your neighbor."

On January 20, 2001 George W. Bush issued a proclamation that pointed us to the 'vertical' aspect of the New Covenant way: love the Lord your God with all your heart, soul, mind, and strength. On January 28ᵗʰ, his three simple words directed us to the 'horizontal' aspect of the New Covenant way: love your neighbor as yourself.

The leadership of the revival in Hezekiah's day included elements of both <u>civil</u> leadership (Hezekiah and the elders of Judah) and <u>religious</u> leadership (Azariah, the high priest, and the priests and Levites). Likewise, in our day, God desires to touch not just the "priests and the Levites" — the believers & Christian leaders — but also some of our secular "elders." God is raising up people to be a part of the fulfillment of His purpose. George W. Bush, I believe, is a picture of many "Bushes," if you will, that God desires to raise up on the local, state and federal level, for the hour in which we live.

THE REVELATION OF HIS CALLING

As believers, we need to pray that George W. Bush would receive a more specific understanding of his calling. I would submit to you that he has a truly sincere heart, but he does not yet have a fully informed heart. George W. Bush wrote an autobiography entitled <u>A Charge to Keep</u>.[24] The title itself comes from the Methodist hymn written by Charles Wesley, "A Charge to Keep I Have." Wesley took the words almost verbatim from a Bible commentary written by Matthew Henry, one of the most well-known and respected of the Puritan Bible scholars.[25] Is it a coincidence that our president's favorite hymn reflects the heart of one of the most godly and influential of all the English Puritan leaders? Is it also a coincidence that George W. Bush is himself of Puritan stock, being a descendant of Robert R. Livingston, a Puritan dissenter who arrived in New England in 1673?[26] Such facts, I believe, are not coincidences, but rather indications that God has, at some level, sown into George W. Bush the heart of our "founding grandfathers," the Puritans. Given the foundational influence of our Puritan forebears on this nation, the significance of this does not elude us, but instead astounds us.

Wesley's hymn begins, "A charge to keep I have, a God to glorify." The back jacket of the president's autobiography pictures a painting loaned to him when he became the governor of Texas. For George W. Bush, that painting captures the message of the hymn. Bush quotes from I Corinthians 4:2, "Now it is required that those who have been given a trust prove faithful." Our president knows he has been given a trust. He knows he has been given a charge. We need to pray that he will come to fully understand what that charge is. A close friend of the President has said in an interview that George W. Bush <u>does</u> believe that he has a calling, as it were, to fight the war on terrorism.[27] The interviewer noted that it is almost as though it is a calling of Biblical proportions. I do not believe the President's *only* calling is to fight the war on terrorism. That is only a small part of his calling. May we pray daily that he will come into a deeper understanding of the full nature of his "charge to keep."

One Saturday morning in February 2001, I was attending a Messianic congregation in Israel. Before the pastor gave his message, he said, "I want to pray today for the President; but not the president of Israel, President Katsav. I want to pray for President George 'W' Bush." He added, "I don't know why I'm supposed to pray for him, but I just know I need to pray for him."

As he mentioned our president's name, I began to weep. The Lord so deeply touched my heart that I found myself on my knees, and then on my face, praying for George W. Bush. As I prayed, the Lord impressed upon me again **how important it is that Christians pray for Bush to fulfill his calling.** I sensed that without a revelation from the Lord, he will miss it!

Then the Lord began to impress upon me Biblical examples from which to pray. I remembered Pharaoh, the secular king of Egypt, to whom God granted revelation through dreams and then provided Joseph as the interpreter. As a result, not only were Jacob and his sons saved, but Egypt and the ancient near East were saved as well. **I prayed, "God, you gave Pharaoh revelation. Give George W. Bush revelation."**

The Holy Spirit then reminded me of Cyrus, the Persian king who issued the decree permitting the Jews to return to Judah after the Babylonian captivity. According to the Jewish historian, Josephus, Cyrus was shown a prophecy with his name in it that had been written by Isaiah 100 years earlier. Josephus wrote that this obvious revelatory miracle convinced Cyrus that he was to issue the decree to let the Jewish people return to Judah.

Next I thought of Peter, the New Testament Apostle first called to share the Gospel with the Gentiles (Acts 10). Through a trance, the Lord gave Peter the same revelation three times, yet he still did not comprehend it. The Lord then interpreted the revelation, explained it, and brought Cornelius's messengers right to Peter's door to confirm His message. After Peter preached the Gospel to Cornelius's household, the Lord poured out His Spirit on them in such a powerful way that Peter knew that it was the Lord at work! Peter told the gentiles gathered at Cornelius's house that if the Lord had not spoken to him so clearly, he would not have entered the house of a gentile. I prayed, "Lord, if the Apostle Peter did not grasp Your revelation apart from Your intervention and explanation, then neither will our president unless You choose to show him the same mercy. Lord, have mercy on him."

Some time later, the Lord showed me a rather interesting Scripture about John the Baptist's recognition of Jesus. Speaking of Jesus, John said, "I would not have known him, except that the one who sent me to baptize with water told me, 'The man on whom you see the Spirit come down and remain is he who will baptize with the Holy Spirit.' " (John 1:33) Even John the Baptist, called to be the forerunner of Jesus, said he would not have recognized Him if the Holy Spirit had not revealed Jesus to him.

While the pastor prayed, I cried out to the Lord, "Speak to George W. Bush! Speak to him through the Word of God! Speak to him in whatever ways You see fit. As you revealed Your will to Pharaoh and Cyrus, pagan men; and to Peter and John, godly men; so reveal Yourself and Your purposes to George W. Bush."

A 'CYRUS' CALLING

As I was praying silently, I heard the pastor pray: **"God, could it be that you would be pleased to raise George W. Bush up as a Cyrus for our [the Jewish] people?"** The Lord powerfully quickened that prayer in my spirit.

In the days that followed, I went to the Word of God to learn more about the life of Cyrus. Was there perhaps something significant the Lord wanted to show me from his life? I was struck by several of the passages concerning Cyrus. In Isaiah 44:28-45:1-4, the Lord says of Cyrus:

'...He is my shepherd and will accomplish all that I please; he will say of Jerusalem, "Let it be rebuilt," and of the temple, "Let its foundations be laid."'

"This is what the Lord says to his anointed, to Cyrus, whose right hand I take hold of to subdue nations before him and to strip kings of their armor, to open doors before him so that gates will not be shut: I will go before you and will level the mountains; I will break down gates of bronze and cut through bars of iron. I will give you the treasures of darkness, riches stored in secret places, so that you may know that I am the LORD, the God of Israel, who summons you by name. For the sake of Jacob my servant, of Israel my chosen, I summon you by name...."

Isaiah 46:11 declares that the Lord would call "from a far-off land a man to fulfill [his] purpose" for Israel. In context, the reference is to Cyrus, the king of Persia. In Isaiah 48:15, the Lord speaks of Cyrus once again, "I, even I, have spoken; yes, I have called him. I will bring him, and he will succeed in his mission."

What do I believe the Lord was trying to show me? **In the past, God used a foreign kingdom and a foreign king to bless Israel, according to His supernatural purposes. Could it be that God would do the same thing again in our day?**

Please do not misunderstand me. I am not saying that these Scriptures were written specifically about George W. Bush — or leaders that might follow in his footsteps — in their original context. Of course, they were not. They were written about the historical Cyrus of Persia. But, could it be that just as Persia blessed the Jewish people — in a way unique among ancient kingdoms mentioned in Scripture — so our nation might bless them as well, in a significant and substantial way, in the day in which we live? Could it be that **just as God raised up Cyrus to bless the Jewish people** and set the tone for succeeding Persian kings, **might He also raise up George W. Bush for the same purpose?** Could it be? I believe so.

Such a scenario would require a miracle, given the direction in which our nation is headed at this point, but our God is a miracle-working God. If he can speak to Biblical figures in the Old and New Testaments, pagans and believers alike, then He can speak to us. If He can speak to the figures of Biblical history and those of Christian history over the last 2000 years, then He can speak to George W. Bush today. Is it also possible that **God could use us** to be part of such a plan, **as we pray** that George W. Bush would have ears to hear, eyes to see, and a spirit to receive what God has for him? Again, I believe the answer is yes.

I believe God has sown a seed in George W. Bush's heart concerning his calling to bless the Jewish people. He is under tremendous pressure from the State Department, the U.N., the E.U, and Arab nations, to compel Israel to concede "land for peace" as part of the Road Map. Yet, at the same time I do believe that God has been and is at work in his heart. George W. Bush went to Israel in 1998. While he was there, two friends of his — one Christian and the other Jewish — went down to the Sea of Galilee, joined hands under the water, and prayed together. At a banquet on their last evening in Israel, Bush's Christian friend related this story. He then shared the words of a hymn brought to remembrance by his experience at the Sea of Galilee. George W. Bush recorded this experience, and the words of this hymn, in his autobiography:

> *Now is the time approaching*
> *By prophets long foretold*
> *When all shall dwell together*
> *One Shepherd, and one fold.*
> *Now Jew and Gentile meeting*
> *From many a distant shore*
> *Around an altar kneeling*
> *One common Lord adore.*[28]

Isn't that amazing? Yes, the Lord has definitely sown a seed in our president's heart concerning God's heart for the Jewish people.

THE JEWS AND A FUTURE "EXODUS" FROM RUSSIA

Isaiah 60:8-10 says, "Who are these that fly along like clouds, like doves to their nests? Surely the islands look to me; in the lead are the ships of Tarshish, bringing your sons from afar....**Foreigners will rebuild your walls, and their kings will serve you....**"

My wife and I lived in Russia from 1991-1998. During those years the Lord spoke to our hearts about a future exodus of the Jewish people in the midst of persecution. In the 1990s the world witnessed a tremendous exodus of the Jewish people from the "Land of the Far North," the former Soviet Union. This exodus was one characterized by freedom and did not take place under duress. But that does not mean it is not significant. It most certainly is. God is fulfilling the word He spoke to Ezekiel that a day would come when He would restore His people, not because of their faithfulness, but for His own name's sake. (Ezekiel 36:22-24) Currently, the Jewish people are living in the land in unbelief. But God, in His faithfulness, and for the sake of His name, is bringing them back to fulfill His purpose. God has initiated a physical and spiritual restoration of Israel and the Jewish people.

Old Testament passages such as Jeremiah 16:14-15 speak of an exodus so great that when it takes place, the Jewish people will no longer talk about the Exodus from Egypt, but rather the Exodus from the "land of the North," and from all the other nations from whence they have come.

> "However, the days are coming," declares the LORD, "when men will no longer say, 'As surely as the LORD lives, who brought the Israelites up out of Egypt,' but they will say, 'As surely as the LORD lives, who brought the Israelites up out of the land of the north and out of all the countries where he had banished them.' For I will restore them to the land I gave their forefathers." (Jeremiah 16:14-15)

As of today, what is still the pivotal historical event for Jewish people, even those who do not believe in God? The Passover, and the Exodus from Egypt! Not the "Exodus from the Land of the Far North," and from all the other nations where they have been scattered. I would submit to you that the ultimate fulfillment of such passages still lies ahead of us.

Right now the relationship between Russia and the United States seems warm and friendly on the surface. But in reality the attitude of the Russian people toward America and the West, and toward democracy and a free market economic system, is not what it once was in the heady days following the collapse of the U.S.S.R. Many of the people reject democracy because they do not understand what it really is. What they have had is <u>not</u> democracy, but they think they have experienced it and found it wanting. They reject a free market economy because they have seen a small percentage of the population get rich while the overwhelming majority has been impoverished. Putin and Bush seem to get along well, but Putin also gets along with world leaders of questionable reputations. He has signed a friendship pact with China. Russia is also helping Iran develop nuclear technology, allegedly for a nuclear power plant. In 2001 the last major independent news outlet in Russia was closed. There is no longer an independent media monitoring the government and the powers that be. As Putin moves to continue to consolidate his power, his would-be opponents end up in jail on questionable charges.

Could it be that the day will come when democracy will collapse in Russia? Will we see an evil hybrid of communism and fascism come to power? A totalitarian regime, perhaps even similar to that of Hitler himself? Interestingly enough, there is a figure similar to Hitler who is rising in prominence and influence in Russia. His name is Alexander Sherbakov. I am not predicting he is going to be the Adolph Hitler of the future. I am merely noting an interesting parallel in history. In the 1920s, Adolph Hitler was considered to be a kook. He tried to overthrow the government, was arrested, and thrown in prison. He was later released and in less than ten years he became the Fuhrer of Germany. In 1993, Boris Yeltsin faced a short-lived coup attempt. You may remember the media pictures of the blackened Russian "White House" in Moscow. Sherbakov actually managed to take control of a TV station for a brief period of time. He was arrested when the coup failed and thrown into prison. After a very conservative parliament was elected, he was released and has since that time been traveling all over Russia preaching Nazism! He is the head of a growing movement known as the Russian National Unity Party. Adherents even wear a Russified version of a swastika on their Nazi uniforms.

Please understand that I am not predicting anything specific about what this one man will do. <u>But I am commenting on the spirit that is on the rise in Russia.</u> Russian nationalism and anti-Semitism are increasing at an alarming rate as the economy continues to deteriorate. I believe that a day will come — I am not saying *when* it will come, specifically — when Russia will return to totalitarianism, and the Jewish people who are already being blamed and scapegoated for Russia's problems will be so all the more. I believe they will be persecuted and forced to leave the former Soviet Union in a massive, frenzied exodus.

Question: Could the U.S. become like the ancient Tarshish mentioned in Isaiah 60? Could our nation be a far away coastland that would spring to Israel's defense in a day of great distress? Could it be that our 'Cyrus' — whether that would be George Bush or another future leader that would nevertheless follow in that same spirit of Cyrus — would authorize American ships and planes, "doves" who fly like a cloud, to come and rescue many Jewish people? To shuttle massive numbers of refugees from the former Soviet Union to Israel — or perhaps temporarily to other countries, to await an orderly entry and absorption into their homeland? I believe the answer is 'yes.'

Certainly this is an issue of tremendous significance and merits further focused prayer for divine confirmation and for strategic wisdom. **What I would like to submit to you is that our president is a special man.** He is most certainly just a man; but he is a man with a sincere heart. I believe our God honors sincere hearts. George W. Bush has not known the Lord for a long time. He has not been taught in churches that would have built into him an appreciation for God's purposes for Israel and the Jewish people or the significance of the covenant land of Israel. Nevertheless, I believe he is a man of integrity; a man who would have ears to hear, if he knew he were hearing from God. He is a man to whom God has given great courage, one who knows he has a commission to fulfill. **What is our role? To pray, "Lord, show George W. Bush what**

his calling is. Show him the full nature of his commission. **Raise him up as a Hezekiah for our nation and as a Cyrus for Israel and the Jewish people."**

These powerful words provided the inspiration for the title of George W. Bush's autobiography. Might I encourage you to turn this hymn into a daily prayer for our president:

A Charge to Keep I Have

A charge to keep I have,
A God to glorify,
A never dying soul to save,
And fit it for the sky.

To serve the present age,
My calling to fulfill;
O may it all my powers engage
To do my Master's will.

Arm me with watchful care
As in Thy sight to live,
And now Thy servant, Lord, prepare
A strict account to give!

Help me to watch and pray,
And still on Thee rely,
O let me not my trust betray,
But press to realms on high.[29]

"O, Lord, a charge to keep he has; a God to glorify. To serve this present age, His calling to fulfill; O may it all his powers engage to do his Master's will. Arm him, Lord, with watchful care, as in Your sight to live; and now Your servant — George W. Bush — prepare a strict account to give. Help him to watch and pray, and let him on Thee rely; and let him not his trust betray, but press to realms on high."

I read in an article in a major national newspaper that George

W. Bush continues to read his Bible and pray every day, even as busy as he is, in the midst of our national crisis.[30] Aides say his Bible is often sitting on his desk in the Oval Office, the highest office in the land! When have we ever heard such a thing reported? One aide said that he often mentions the Scriptures he is reading in meetings with staff. He reportedly opens every cabinet meeting with prayer.

George W. Bush is not the answer to our problems. He is not our Savior — God is. Please do not mishear me! But **God uses men.** George W. Bush has a calling to keep. And so do we. May we rise up and be found faithful.

A PRAYER IN RESPONSE

Lord Jesus, we have a charge to keep. We have a God to glorify. Our president does, and we do, too. May we be sons and daughters of Issachar, who understand the times and know what to do, and how to pray. May our president be one as well. May he, too, know what to do, and how to pray. O, Lord, would You speak to him, and would You reveal to him Your will. Speak to him about his calling as a Hezekiah, and as a Cyrus. Supernaturally confirm it, Lord, according to Your perfect wisdom. May he receive Your word in awe and wonder. May the fear of God fall on him. May he embrace his calling by faith, and, by Your grace, would he obey with the shrewdness of a serpent and the innocence of a dove. Fulfill Your purposes for him, and for our nation, in this hour of history. Lord Jesus, be glorified in George W. Bush. Be glorified in us as well. May You receive all the praise and glory. Amen.

CHAPTER SEVEN

Is God Finished with the Jewish People?

"Sons of Issachar for the 21st Century" — that is the theme of this book. What does it mean for us as Christians to be sons of Issachar in this century? Certainly we must understand God's heart for our own country in the days ahead. Only then will we know how to pray and what to do. The American Church and the American nation are at a crossroads. How we respond is crucial. The first several chapters of this book have been devoted to these topics.

Yet to be sons of Issachar, we must also look beyond our borders to see what God is doing in the rest of the world today. In the last few decades we have witnessed a resurgent Israel as well as a revival of fundamentalist Islam. The Arab nations of the Middle East and the Jewish state of Israel seem to be on a collision course. Fundamentalist Muslims will not rest until Israel, the "Little Satan," is destroyed. The United States, termed the "Big Satan" by Islamic extremists, stands in the way. Usama bin Laden has said two reasons for the September 11th attacks were the U.S. military presence in the Persian Gulf and U.S. support for Israel.

UNDERSTANDING OUR TIMES
To be sons of Issachar in our generation, we must have a better

understanding of these issues. What is the significance of the rebirth of the modern state of Israel? How do we understand the renascence of Islam in this hour? Clearly, a spiritual battle is raging in the heavenly places, and we must understand it in order to pray effectively.

How important is it that the United States support Israel? Is there any Biblical significance to the re-establishment of the state of Israel, or is its re-emergence a mere coincidence? Is God finished with the Jewish people? Or, as a people, do they still have a purpose in God's plans as we look to the future? How should the Church relate to Israel and the Jewish people?

Is Islam a religion of peace? What are the goals of Islam? How do we understand this religion and what can we expect in the generation ahead?

Both of these topics are of great concern to us as American Christians. We cannot afford to stick our heads in the sand and wait for the all controversy to blow over. We find ourselves in the midst of the cosmic spiritual battle of our age. It is imperative that we understand these issues so that we will know how to pray with confidence and respond with courage. In the next several chapters we will explore these pressing questions. May the Lord give us His heart and His wisdom.

GOD AND THE JEWISH PEOPLE

What does Scripture tell us about God's relationship to Israel? What exactly did God promise to Abraham and his descendants? What is the nature of the covenant God made with Abraham? Does it still stand today? These questions will be the focus of this chapter. They are significant themes in and of themselves, but they are also preparation for what we will turn our attention to in the next few chapters. The next chapters will address the response of the Body of Christ, particularly the Gentile Body, to the Jewish people. How are we, as Gentiles, to relate to Israel and the Jewish people? How has the Church related to the Jews throughout history?

Then we will examine the epic battle facing our world today: militant Islam vs. Christianity. The battle, of course, is ultimately a spiritual one, a battle not with flesh and blood, but with the principalities and powers behind Islam. Powers that are coming not only against Israel and the Jewish people, but also against "Christendom." As I noted earlier, many Muslims view America as the "Great Satan," and Israel as the "Little Satan." This is not fundamentally a geopolitical conflict, but rather a spiritual conflict which has great bearing on the Church and on our nation in the generation ahead.

IS GOD FINISHED WITH THE JEWISH PEOPLE?

So we ask these very important questions for today: **Is God finished with the Jewish people?** What about the modern state of Israel? Is its founding the fulfillment of Biblical prophecy? Or is it merely a coincidence that Israel is back in the land?

To answer these questions, we must first look at the Abrahamic covenant. In Genesis 12, God called Abraham to leave Ur of the Chaldees and travel to a land that the Lord said He would show him. The Lord said in Genesis 12:7 that He would give Abraham that land as a gift. In Genesis 13 Abraham offered Lot what was then the choice land. (It was later consumed in the fiery judgment on Sodom and Gomorrah.) Abraham then took the less-appealing land, from a natural perspective. The Lord then spoke to Abraham again, saying, "Lift up your eyes from where you are and look north and south, east and west. All the land that you see I will give you and your offspring **forever**...Go, walk through the length and breadth of the land, for I am giving it to you." (Genesis 13:14-15, 17) [Emphasis added]

GOD'S UNILATERAL COVENANT

Genesis 15 records the covenant-cutting ceremony between God and Abraham. Such a ceremony was very common in the ancient world at that time. The two covenanting parties would gather the animals as described in Genesis 15, slice them in two, and then the two parties would walk between the animals. This act signified the solemnity of the agreement and the commitment of each party to one another and to the pact. What is most interesting about this covenant-cutting ceremony in Genesis 15 is that the Lord alone passed between the animals. Abraham did not. The Lord thereby indicated that this was God's covenant, and that He would assume the responsibility for its administration. The Lord was the promising party, and **His oath was unilateral and unconditional.**

Note that in Genesis 15 there are no requirements of Abraham, other than that he believe, which of course he did.

In Genesis 17:7-11, God established circumcision as the sign of the covenant:

> " 'I will establish my covenant as an **everlasting covenant** between me and you and your descendants after you for the generations to come, to be your God and the God of your descendants after you. The whole land of Canaan, where you are now an alien, I will give as an **everlasting possession** to you and your descendants after you; and I will be their God.' Then God said to Abraham, 'As for you, you must keep my covenant, you and your descendants after you for the generations to come. This is my covenant with you and your descendants after you, the covenant that you are to keep: Every male among you shall be circumcised. You are to undergo circumcision, and it will be the sign of the covenant between me and you....' " [Emphasis added]

This is a covenant that Abraham kept, and a covenant that the Jewish people have kept from that day to this.

In Genesis 26:3-5, **the Lord <u>affirmed to Isaac</u>** the promise and the covenant that He had unilaterally made with Abraham:

> "For to you and your descendants I will give all these lands and will confirm **the oath I swore** to your father Abraham. I will make your descendants as numerous as the stars in the sky and will give them all these lands, and through your offspring all nations of the earth shall be blessed, **because Abraham obeyed me**, and kept my requirements, my commands, my decrees and my laws." [Emphasis added]

The Lord once again affirmed the Abrahamic covenant **<u>to Jacob</u>** in Genesis 35:12: "The land I gave to Abraham and Isaac I also give to you, and I will give this land to your descendants after you."

What land is at issue in the Abrahamic Covenant? What land exactly was <u>God</u> talking about? Genesis 15:18 offers a clear answer to this question: "On that day the Lord made a covenant with Abram and said, "To your descendants I give this land from the river of Egypt" [the Nile] "to the great river the Euphrates." In Joshua 1:4 the Lord said, "Your territory will extend from the desert [again, in Egypt] to Lebanon [in the north], from the great river, the Euphrates — all the Hittite country — to the Great Sea on the west [the Mediterranean Sea]."

What I submit to you is that God **unilaterally and unconditionally made a covenant with Abraham.** As a part of this covenant, He gave Abraham a gift. The gift was God's covenant land, the land that He promised as the land of Israel. The Lord reaffirmed the promise both to Isaac and to Jacob, granting Abraham and his descendants the **title** to the land.

At Mt. Sinai, Moses reminded the Lord of the unilateral covenant He had made with Abraham, Isaac, and Jacob. After the Israelites had sinned against God by worshipping the golden calf, the Lord threatened to destroy the Israelites and make Moses into a great nation. Moses, the great intercessor that he was, pleaded with the Lord to turn from his fierce anger and forgive Israel's sin:

> Remember your servants Abraham, Isaac, and Israel, to whom you swore by your own self: 'I will make your descendants as numerous as the stars in the sky and I will give your descendants all this land I promised them and it will be their inheritance forever.' (Exodus 33:13)

THE LAND: TITLE vs. POSSESSION

Through the Mosaic covenant, the Lord did, however, lay out the conditions for continuous **possession** of the land. If the Israelites obeyed, there would be blessing. If they disobeyed, there would be curses. If they persisted in disobedience, they would even be uprooted from the land and dispersed.

Just as it pleased the LORD to make you prosper and increase in number, so it will please him to ruin and destroy you. You will be uprooted from the land you are entering to possess. Then the LORD will scatter you among all nations, from one end of the earth to the other. There you will worship other gods....Among those nations you will find no repose, no resting place for the sole of your foot. There the LORD will give you an anxious mind, eyes weary with longing, and a despairing heart. You will live in constant suspense, filled with dread both night and day, never sure of your life. In the morning you will say, 'If only it were evening!' and in the evening, 'If only it were morning!' — because of the terror that will fill your hearts and the sights that your eyes will see. (Deuteronomy 28:63-67)

History has born witness to God's faithfulness to His covenant, including the conditions He gave for the **possession** of the land.

What is of utmost importance as we look at this issue is to be very careful to distinguish between title and possession. We can have a title to something, but not possession of it.

The above verses were indeed a preview of the history of the Jewish people! Not only during the Babylonian captivity, but over the last 2,000 years. The Jewish people have found no repose among the nations. They have indeed been filled with anxiety and dread throughout their history.

The ten northern tribes of Israel were utterly dispersed in 722 BC by the Assyrians. The two southern tribes, Judah and Benjamin, were then dispersed by the Babylonians in 586 BC. Finally, after the national Jewish rejection of the Messiah, the Romans conquered Jerusalem in 70 AD, and the Great Diaspora began, one that would last almost 2,000 years. Yet — and this is of utmost significance — notice that nowhere in Deuteronomy 28 did the Lord say that He would revoke the title to the land; just the possession of it. **If God had said that, it would have violated the covenant that he had made with Abraham, in which He had unilaterally promised the land as an "everlasting possession to Abraham and his**

descendants."

In fact, the Lord actually affirmed the **everlasting nature of the covenant** He made with Abraham in several passages:

I Chronicles 16:15-18

He remembers his covenant forever,
the word he commanded, for a thousand generations,
the covenant he made with Abraham,
the oath he swore to Isaac.
He confirmed it to Jacob as a decree,
to Israel as an **everlasting** covenant:
'To you I will give the land of Canaan
as the portion you will inherit.' [Emphasis added]

Jeremiah 31:35-37

This is what the LORD says,
he who appoints the sun
to shine by day,
who decrees the moon and stars
to shine by night,
who stirs up the sea
so that its waves roar —
the LORD Almighty is his name:
'Only if these decrees [by which the Lord reigns over nature!]
vanish from my sight,'
declares the Lord,
'will the descendants of Israel ever cease
to be a nation before me.'
This is what the LORD says:
'Only if the heavens above can be measured
and the foundations of the earth below be searched out
will I reject all the descendants of Israel
because of all they have done,'
declares the Lord. [Emphasis added]

On the one hand, the prophet Jeremiah prophesied that God's judgment was irrevocable: the Jews would be carried away to captivity in Babylon. Yet, the Lord also spoke through Jeremiah that regardless of what they had done, He would not reject them permanently.

Jeremiah 33:24-26

"Have you noticed that these people are saying [the Lord is speaking], 'The LORD has rejected the two kingdoms He chose'? So they despise my people and no longer regard them as a nation. This is what the LORD says: 'If I have not established my covenant with day and night and the fixed laws of heaven and earth, then I will reject the descendants of Jacob and David my servant and will not choose one of his sons to rule over the descendants of Abraham, Isaac and Jacob. For I will restore their fortunes, and I will have compassion on them.' "

In **Zechariah 2:8**, the Lord speaks concerning nations that had come against Israel, even nations that He had used in some instances to discipline her. Nevertheless, He makes the very interesting comment: "For whoever touches you touches the apple of his [God's] eye." Despite Israel's failures and her disobedience, she is still special and beloved because the Lord chose to love her.

The Apostle Paul asks in **Romans 11:1**:

I ask then, did God reject his people? By no means!...Again I ask: did they stumble so as to fall beyond recovery? Not at all! Rather, because of their transgression, salvation has come to the Gentiles, to make Israel envious....**"For God's gifts and his call are irrevocable."** (Romans 11:1, 11, 29) [Emphasis Added]

The context of this Scripture directly concerns Israel. God's call for Israel is irrevocable. Disobedience under the Mosaic Covenant did not annul the Abrahamic Covenant. Paul confirms this vitally important fact in **Galatians 3:17-18**: "What I mean is this: The law, introduced 430 years later, does not set aside the covenant previously established by God and thus do away with the promise. For if the inheritance depends on the law, then it no longer depends on the promise, but God in his grace gave it to Abraham through a promise." What promise? The promise made to Abraham that the Lord would give him:

a *people* (the Israelites),

a *place* (the covenant land of Israel), and

a *purpose* (to bless all men through him);
and that these promises would be kept

in perpetuity. [31]

God has been faithful to His covenants. **Israel lost possession of the land in 722 BC and in 586 BC** because of disobedience under the Mosaic Covenant. After the nation rejected the Messiah, the Jews were once again dispersed in 70 AD, when the Romans conquered Jerusalem. **Yet, the Lord has never revoked Israel's <u>title</u> to the land!**

Jesus Himself prophesied in Luke 21:24 that the Jews would be taken captive to the nations, and that Jerusalem would be trampled on until the times of the Gentiles are fulfilled. History has testified to Jesus' words as different powers have controlled the land: the Romans, the Byzantines, the Persians, the Arabs, the Crusaders, the Marmelukes, the Turks, the British, and the Jordanians. Then, on June 7, 1967, Israel liberated the Jewish Quarter, gaining control of all of Jerusalem for the first time in 2,000 years. When Israeli forces reached the Wailing Wall — all that remains of the Temple of Jesus' day — the chief Rabbi of the Israeli Defense Force declared, "We are entering the Messianic era for the Jewish people." [32] What a very interesting statement indeed! There was definitely something significant in the mind and heart of the Jewish people about 1967. (Later, we will return to the significance of the year 1967 for Israel and for the Body of Christ.)

"EXODUS II"

After almost 2,000 years the Diaspora began to come to an end in 1948 with the establishment of the modern State of Israel. Is Israel back in the land by God's design? Or, is its creation a mere coincidence? **Does the Church have a responsibility, or even a calling, to bless the Jewish people, and even Israel herself?** To answer these questions, we must look to Old Testament prophecies concerning God's promised restoration of Israel.

Isaiah 43:5-6:

"Do not be afraid, for I am with you. I will bring your children from the east and gather you from the west. I will say to the north, 'Give them up!' and to the south, 'Do not hold them back.' Bring my sons from afar and my daughters from the ends of the earth."

Significantly, this passage pictures the Jewish people returning to the land from all directions. Some believers say that such prophecies for Israel's restoration refer only to that which took place after the Babylonian captivity. But if that is the case, why are they coming from all directions? North, south, east and west. I find most intriguing the Lord's statement, "I will say to the north, 'Give them up!'" The Lord is <u>commanding</u> them to be given up.

I would like to suggest that there is a very interesting parallel between that prophecy and what we have seen over the last 15 years in the former Soviet Union. Prior to the collapse of communism, most Jewish people were forbidden to leave the USSR, the "land of the far north." Then suddenly, communism miraculously fell; no one predicted it. Historians and politicians were caught off guard. The walls came down, and since that time approximately one million Jewish people have returned to the state of Israel. **Is this a coincidence? Or the fulfillment of Biblical prophecy?**

Jeremiah 16:14-16:

"However, the days are coming," declares the Lord, "when men will no longer say, 'As surely as the LORD lives who brought the Israelites up out of Egypt,' but they will say, 'As surely as the LORD lives, who brought the Israelites up out of the land of the north and out of all the countries where he had banished them.' **For I will restore them to the land I gave their forefathers**." [Emphasis added]

Jeremiah 23:7-8:

"So then, the days are coming," declares the LORD, "when people will no longer say, 'As surely as the LORD lives, who brought the Israelites up out of Egypt,' but they will say, 'As surely as the LORD lives, who brought the descendants of Israel up out of the land of the north and out of all the countries where he had banished them.' **Then they will live in their own land**." [Emphasis added]

What is profound about these Scriptures is that they prophesy a return that will become so great in the eyes of the Jewish people, that it will supplant the Exodus from Egypt as the pivotal event of their history. For 3,500 years the centerpiece of history for the Jewish people has been the Passover. Even for the most secular of Jews, the Passover is deeply embedded in their spiritual consciousness. I believe we have yet to see this greatest "Exodus," as these Scriptures prophesy. "From the land of the north, the far north, and from all of the nations." Did you know that there are approximately 12,000,000 Jewish people who currently live outside the state of Israel? Only 5,000,000 Jewish people live in Israel. Twelve million-plus live "among the nations," still scattered to the four corners of the earth.

Amos 9:14-15:

"I will bring back my exiled people Israel; they will rebuild the ruined cities and live in them. They will plant vineyards and drink their wine; they will make gardens and eat their fruit. **I will plant Israel in their own land, never again to be uprooted from the land I have given them."** [Emphasis added]

God says unequivocally, "I will plant Israel in her own land, never again to be uprooted from the land I have given her." Have we seen such a <u>final</u> return of the Jewish people? No! I believe Scripture clearly teaches that we have not.

I would like to emphasize two key points that emerge from all these Scriptures. First of all, the scope of these prophecies could not have been completely fulfilled with the very limited return from captivity in Babylon. A small remnant came with Zerubbabel, and later a small remnant came with Ezra. Could we look at these historical returns as **"a"** fulfillment? A partial fulfillment of these prophecies? Yes, most definitely! But a **complete** fulfillment? I do not believe so. The prophet Ezekiel speaks of a day when Israel will be regathered to the land to such an extent that not one will be left behind (39:28). We have never seen that! But I believe that God, faithful to His word, will do it!

Secondly, **Israel's restoration — both physically and spiritually — is a process**. Not just one event, but many events, as God works out His purposes through history.

Ezekiel 36:22-28, 32:

"Therefore say to the house of Israel, 'This is what the Sovereign LORD says: It is not for your sake, O house of Israel, that I am going to do these things, but for the sake of my holy name, which you have profaned among the nations where you have gone. I will show the holiness of my great name, which has been profaned among the nations, the name you profaned among them. Then the nations will know that I am the LORD, declares the Sovereign LORD, when I show myself holy through you before their eyes. **For I will take you out of the nations; I will gather you from all the countries and bring you**

back into your own land. I will sprinkle clean water on you, and you will be clean; I will cleanse you from all your impurities and from all your idols. I will give you a new heart and put a new spirit in you; I will remove from you your heart of stone and give you a heart of flesh. And I will put my Spirit in you and move you to follow my decrees and be careful to keep my laws. You will live in the land I gave your forefathers; you will be my people, and I will be your God....I want you to know that **I am not doing this for your sake**," declares the Sovereign LORD. "Be ashamed and disgraced for your conduct, O house of Israel!" [Emphasis added]

What we see in this passage, particularly in verses 24 and 25, is a process. The Lord is basically saying, "I will regather you physically, and <u>then</u> I will pour out my Spirit on you." A physical restoration will precede a spiritual restoration. Note that the Lord will not do this because Israel deserves it. Currently, Israel — as a nation — is still in unbelief, rejecting her Messiah. But the Lord will accomplish His purpose for His name's sake. The Lord is faithful to His word, and He does what He promises.

Ezekiel 37:1-2, 11, 21-22, 25:

"The hand of the LORD was upon me, and he brought me out by the Spirit of the LORD and set me in the middle of a valley; it was full of bones. He led me back and forth among them, and I saw a great many bones on the floor of the valley, bones that were very dry....Then he said to me: 'Son of man, these bones are the whole house of Israel. They say, "Our bones are dried up and our hope is gone; we are cut off.'...'This is what the Sovereign Lord says: I will take the Israelites out of the nations where they have gone. I will gather them from all around and **bring them back into their own land. <u>I will make them one nation in the land, on the mountains of Israel</u>.** There will be one king over all of them and they will

never again be two nations or be divided into two kingdoms....They will live in the land I gave to my servant
Jacob, the land where your fathers lived. They and their
children and their children's children will live there
forever, and David my servant will be their prince
forever.'" [Emphasis added]

Once again history has borne out the words of the prophet
Ezekiel. For her disobedience, Israel — both in Biblical history and
from the New Testament era forward — has been dispersed, as was
prophesied in Deuteronomy 28. Yet, in spite of it all, the Jewish
people have been miraculously preserved. What other ethnic group,
without any continual attachment to some piece of land — whether
its own nation or a geographic area in a particular nation — has
ever been able to maintain its own national identity, culture, religion, and language?

TRACING ISRAEL'S RESTORATION
Around the turn of the last century, after almost 2,000 years of
dispersion, God began to move very dramatically to initiate this
process of restoration physically and, of course, spiritually. What
happened? Let's survey the high spots:

1897 — Theodore Hertzl convened the first Jewish congress in
Basel, Switzerland. This unbelieving man predicted that within 50
years there would be a state in the land of Israel for the Jewish
people.

1914-1918 World War I — God moved sovereignly and miraculously among the nations to give Great Britain control of the
Palestinian Mandate. What had belonged to the Ottoman Empire
now belonged to Great Britain. On November 2, 1917, Lord
Balfour, the Foreign Minister of Great Britain, issued what is
known as the Balfour Declaration: "His Majesty's Government
views with favor the establishment in Palestine of the national home
for the Jewish people, and will use their best endeavor to facilitate
the achievement of this object."

1920's/1930's — Because of fear of Arab reprisals, Britain restricted immigration of the Jewish people to their homeland. European Jewry became trapped with no place to go.

World War II — This global struggle was a tragedy for the whole world, but especially for the Jews who suffered the unspeakable horrors of the Holocaust. Six million Jewish men, women, and children were exterminated for no other reason than that they were Jewish. **If God does not have a purpose for the Jewish people, then why is the enemy so set on their destruction?** What other ethnic group has been so relentlessly pursued by enemies throughout history? I believe our evil adversary saw what most in the Church at that point did not see: God was beginning to move! The enemy knew about the conference in Basel. The enemy knew about the Balfour Declaration. The enemy could see what was coming, and he wanted to try to play an "ace," and annihilate the Jewish people before they could ever be restored to the Land, thereby thwarting the fulfillment of God's prophecies. The Lord God, however, is so great and so awesome. He is never taken by surprise. He trumps every ace. As horrible as the Holocaust was, it did grant the Jewish people sympathy in the eyes of the world, if only for a brief window of time. But God used that sympathy and favor to achieve His own purposes....

November 29th, 1947 — The United Nations voted to re-establish the State of Israel as a nation. In one day, at one moment in time, the UN "created" the modern state of Israel. I believe this decision was a fulfillment of **Isaiah 66:8**: "Who has ever heard of such a thing? Who has ever seen such things? Can a country be born in a day or a nation be brought forth in a moment?"

May 1948 through the present day — Israel declared her independence on May 14, 1948, and then the wars began. She fought a war for independence, against five Arab nations that surrounded her, just to secure her statehood. Since that time she has faced her enemies over and over again. Yet, God has miraculously preserved Israel in 1948, 1956, 1967, 1973, 1982, and in 1991. Israel has been preserved against overwhelming odds! A few million Jews, among a sea of hostile Arabs, bent on her destruction. **Is her survival a coincidence? Or a miracle?**

THE SIGNIFICANCE OF 1967

Earlier I mentioned Jesus' prophecy that Jerusalem would be in the hands of the Gentile powers until the time of the Gentiles were fulfilled. (Luke 21:24) What, if any, is the significance of June 7th, 1967, for the Jewish people and the world? The June 21st, 1971 issue of Time magazine featured an article on the "Jesus Movement." [33] Three times, the writer dates the beginning of the movement to 1967. It was during the Jesus movement that Jewish people began to come to know the Lord in larger numbers. In fact, many of the leaders in the Messianic Jewish movement today were saved during the Jesus Movement.[34] In 1967, there were an estimated 2,000 Jewish believers in Jesus, worldwide.[35] A conservative estimate puts that number at 250,000 or more today. **More Jewish people have come to know the Lord since 1967 than from the 4th century to 1967. Read that sentence again. Take a moment and let the weight of that statement wash over you. Is this a coincidence? Or is God beginning to move in a fresh way among His people?**

An article in *Charisma* magazine in 1990 cited a survey that suggested that more than a million Jews in the U.S. alone express "some sort of faith in Y'shua." (Y'shua is Jesus' name in Hebrew.) Perhaps not saving faith, but some sort of acceptance of Y'shua.[36] In 1967 there were no Messianic Jewish congregations in the world. There are now 81 in Israel alone, and according to *Christianity Today,* over 350 throughout the world.[37]

Don Finto, in his book, Your People Shall Be My People, cites the following statistics: "We are told that over half the people who have ever lived on the earth since the days of Adam and Eve are alive today. The latest figures indicate that one out of every five of these is a believer — more believers today than in all the years preceding us. Millions of people on every continent are coming to faith — the greatest revival in the history of the world." [38]

Seventy percent of all those who have ever come to faith in Jesus have come since the first Zionist Conference in

Basel, Switzerland in 1897.... [At that time] the ratio of believers to unbelievers [in the world] was 1 to 27. Today that number is 1 to 5....Over 50 percent of those who have ever come to faith, have come since the founding of the state of Israel in 1948.[39]

We have witnessed not only a geometric increase in population, but also a geometric multiplication of the power of the Holy Spirit in saving the peoples of the earth. According to the Center for World Mission in California, the number of evangelicals is growing at a rate 3.5 times faster than the world's population. More Muslims have trusted Christ since 1980 than in all the previous 1,000 years. The body of Christ is growing worldwide at a rate of 6.9% annually.[40]

The Apostle Paul said in **Romans 11:12, 15**: "But if their transgression means riches for the world, and their loss means riches for the Gentiles, how much greater riches will their fullness bring!...For if their rejection is the reconciliation of the world, what will their acceptance be but life from the dead?" Is history not testifying to the fact that as God moves to restore Israel, there is also a mighty outpouring of the Spirit among the nations?

C.H. Spurgeon summed it up well:

> **I think we do not attach enough importance to the restoration of the Jews**....But certainly, if there is anything promised in the Bible, it is this....**The day shall yet come when the Jews,** who were the first apostles to the Gentiles, the first missionaries to us who were afar off, **shall be gathered in again.** Until that shall be, the fullness of the church's glory can never come. **Matchless benefits to the world are bound up with the restoration of Israel, their gathering shall be as life from the dead.**[41] [Emphasis Added]

Is what we have witnessed over the last 50 years a coincidence? Is this unprecedented move of God among the Jewish people, the likes of which has not been seen for 1,500 years, a coincidence? Is it a coincidence that at the same time God has also been moving among the Gentile nations in a way such as has never been seen before? Or, is this convergence indeed part of the plan of God? I believe the answer is clear.

How do we respond? In awe and with prayer.

A PRAYER IN RESPONSE

Holy One of Israel, we pray for:

1. *The physical restoration of Israel: for the reclamation of the Land, as well as the continued return of Jewish people from the four corners of the earth.*

2. *The spiritual restoration of the Jewish people; that the veil will be removed and multitudes of Jewish people will embrace their Messiah.*

3. *The Church to enter into new understanding of Israel's place in Your purposes.*

4. *Christians to become aware of, and lay aside, any vestiges of anti-Semitic attitudes or ways of thinking in regard to the Jewish people.*

5. *A "Ruth remnant" of the Church in all nations to arise and bless the Jewish people as they return home in the future.*

6. *Reconciliation in the Body between Jewish believers and Gentile believers, and for the emergence in our day of the "one new man" (according to Ephesians 2), Jew and Gentile, in Christ together, the dividing wall of hostility removed.*

7. *A "life from the dead" awakening to sweep the globe as result of Jewish/Gentile reconciliation in the Body, the emergence of a "one new man" testimony, and the restoration of the Jewish people.*

All this we ask for the great glory of Jesus, the King of the Jews, who also is the King of the Gentiles. Thank You that He came not just to rule over us, but to bless us and to enfranchise us. Glory to God for Your marvelous mercy and grace upon us. In Jesus' name, Amen.

CHAPTER EIGHT

The 'Ruth' Remnant
of the Church

One of the most beautiful love stories of the Bible is tucked between the Old Testament books of Joshua and Judges. It is, of course, the story of Ruth and Boaz. The story of the Moabitess who marries into the tribe of Judah and becomes an ancestor of Jesus. The story is often noted for its expression of God's heart for the Gentiles. A picture of a future reality when Gentiles — along with the Jews — would become the bride of our Kinsman-Redeemer.

But, could there be more to the story? Could there be a truth, hidden in this love story, which is relevant for us today? A message, perhaps, for us Gentiles as to how God would have us relate to His chosen people, the Jews? I would like to suggest that this historical narrative is also rich with symbolism that speaks to the Church of our day about our relationship with Israel and the Jewish people. Let us explore this book and mine its precious riches for both Gentile believers and for the Jews.

THE STORY OF NAOMI AND THE HISTORY OF THE JEWS

I will first introduce the cast of characters, and then we will be ready to take a unique look at this special book. I believe that **in Naomi we see a symbol of Israel, the Jewish people.** Her name means "my pleasantness," or "my joy." Her husband's name, Elimelech, means "My God the king." Her son Mahlon's name means "weak" or "sickly," and that of his brother Kilion means "wasting away" or "pining." "Ruth" means "friendship" or "companion," and Boaz, the kinsman-redeemer's name, means "in Him is strength."

Naomi's marriage to Elimelech, whose name means "My God the King," pictures Israel's covenantal relationship with God. Unfortunately, as we read in the book of Ruth, the state of the relationship is not as God intended it. It is no coincidence that the story takes place during the days of the Judges, when "everyone did what was right in his own eyes." (Judges 21:25 NKJV) This period was one of spiritual apostasy, characterized by religious and moral decay. The Israelites were continually attacked and harassed by other nations, an experience similar to that of the Jewish people in the Diaspora since 70 A.D.

Naomi and her family left Bethlehem during a time of famine in search of bread. In the Old Testament, a spiritual famine often preceded a physical famine. When the Israelites turned from the Lord, He brought many types of judgment, one of them being a famine on the land. Likewise, having rejected Jesus, the bread of life, who was born in the "house of bread," Bethlehem *[Hebrew: "beit lechem," or "house of bread"]*, the Jewish people have known a spiritual famine for almost 2,000 years. In the midst of a famine — both physical and spiritual — Naomi and Elimelech left the "house of bread" and looked elsewhere for sustenance. Was Moab the place to look? No! In the same way, the Jewish people have rejected Jesus as their Messiah, and as a result, they have been looking for "bread" in all the wrong places for 2,000 years.

According to the book of Ruth, Elimelech dies in the land of Moab. I stated earlier that I believe Elimelech pictures "My God the king." Of course, God cannot die, but figuratively speaking, it was as though there was a death in the relationship. There was a break, a severing, a separation. This weak relationship with God is pictured in the fruit of the marriage of Naomi and Elimelech, her earthly husband. Their children's names were Mahlon, "weak" and "sickly," and Kilion, "pining away" or "wasting away." That is what we have seen, historically and spiritually, if we examine the lot of the Jewish people over the last 2,000 years. Though miraculously preserved by God, they have nevertheless pined away in many nations.

Instead of turning to the Lord in a time of famine, Naomi and her family abandoned the house of bread, searching for food elsewhere. How awesome that in spite of all this, the Lord beckons Naomi home. In the midst of her affliction, He brings her back to Judah, ultimately that she might be reconnected to her kinsman-redeemer, Boaz. Miraculously, we have seen that same "beckoning" in regard to the Jewish people over the last 100 years, and particularly since 1948 and 1967. Even though Israel is still in the midst of a spiritual famine in the Diaspora, God is beckoning her home. Why? So that she, too, might be reconnected to her Kinsman-Redeemer.

Naomi sets out for home, accompanied by Orpah and Ruth. Each daughter-in-law pictures a type of Gentile. Ruth, whose name means "friend" or "companion," binds her heart to Naomi, to her people, and to her God. Ruth, I believe, pictures a remnant in the Church with an understanding of God's heart for the Jewish people, a remnant committed to loving, supporting, and blessing the Jewish people.

Orpah, on the other hand, does not understand the significance of her identification with Naomi, and returns home to Moab. The opportunity to bless her mother-in-law is lost. Likewise, throughout Church history, most gentile Christians have not understood what it means to be grafted into the olive tree (Romans 11:17), and enfranchised into the commonwealth of Israel (Ephesians 2:11-19). Sadly, as a result, the Church has missed countless opportunities to lovingly provoke the Jewish people to a godly jealousy (Romans 11:11, 13).

Once back in the Land, Naomi tells the women of Bethlehem, "Don't call me Naomi....Call me Mara, because the Almighty has made my life very bitter. I went away full, but the Lord has brought me back empty....The LORD has afflicted me; the Almighty has brought misfortune upon me." (Ruth 1:20-21) Significantly, that is true of the history of the Jewish people. As they look back over 2,000 years in the Diaspora, many Jewish people say, "Forget about being the 'Chosen People.' If this is what it means to be 'chosen,' we don't want to have any part of it!" Golda Meir, the late Prime Minister of Israel, once said, "Lord, can't you choose some other people?" [42]

Because of such intense affliction and persecution throughout history, the majority of Jewish people are overwhelmingly secular. Many are embittered by what they perceive to be God's failure and His rejection of them. In fact, many are atheists or agnostics.

RUTH'S LOVE FOR NAOMI — AN EXAMPLE FOR THE GENTILE CHURCH

After Naomi and Ruth return to Bethlehem, Ruth begins to glean in Boaz's fields. It is because of Naomi's connection to her kinsman-redeemer that Ruth finds favor in the eyes of Boaz. Likewise, we, as Gentiles, owe the Jewish people a great debt. Just as Ruth came to Boaz through Naomi, so we have come to our Messiah through the Jewish people. The Word of God comes to us through the Jewish people. Every author is Jewish except one (Luke). The rest of the Bible is written by Jewish people. Our Messiah, Himself Jewish, is presented, especially in the book of Matthew, as the King of the Jews. We have been blessed by God through a Jewish people, through a predominantly Jewish book, and through a completely Jewish Messiah.

Yet, at the same time, it is Ruth's union with Boaz — who pictures Jesus, our Redeemer — that blesses Naomi and restores her faith. Clearly there is a mutual blessing in this relationship. Blessing for Naomi (the Jewish people) and blessing for Ruth (the Gentiles), through our joint Kinsman-Redeemer, Jesus. In contrast with that of Naomi and Elimelech, the fruit of Ruth and Boaz's union is not weak or sickly; it is Obed, whose name means "servant." Is there any higher calling than to be a servant of the Lord? Does not Philippians 2:7 say that Jesus Himself took the very nature of a servant? What does Paul continually refer to himself as throughout the New Testament, but the servant, the bond-slave, of the Lord Jesus Christ?

Just as God used a Gentile as part of His purpose to restore and nourish Naomi, could it also be a part of His plan to use us, a "Ruth remnant" among Gentile believers, to help reconnect the Jewish people with their Kinsman-Redeemer? To be a part of God's plan to draw the Jewish people back to their Messiah? So that as a result there will be multitudes of Jewish "Obeds" arising? Jewish servants of the Lord, just like Saul, the Jew, who became Paul, the apostle, the servant of the Lord.

In the previous chapter I noted the amazing things God has been doing all over the globe during the last generation. The world has witnessed an unprecedented move of God among the Jewish people, on the one hand, and an unprecedented move of God among unreached nations and people groups on the other. Somehow these phenomena are connected in the heart of God. As Gentile believers, we have a momentous choice before us in the generation ahead. As we look at the time and season in which God has graced us to live, our choice is this: **will we be like Orpah, or will we be like Ruth?** Which type of Gentile will we be? What will our attitude be towards the Jewish people? Remember, Paul said that the Gospel is for the Jew first, and then for the Gentile (Romans 1:16). The Gospel is indeed for everyone, but for the Jew first, and then for the Gentile.

Even as God moves so powerfully to deal with Israel in our generation, will we ignore what he is doing with His people? Will we look upon the Jewish people with contempt? Or, will we choose to embrace them, love them, and bless them in whatever way the Lord might lead us in our circles of influence? It was Ruth, a foreigner, who so loved Naomi that the Bible says she was "better to Naomi than seven sons." Ponder the significance of that statement in the culture of that day, when to have a son was everything! Ruth so loved Naomi that she was "better... than seven sons." (Ruth 4:15) If God could use such a woman to love Naomi and bless her to life again, could He not do the same thing again? Could He use us as Ruths, to lovingly draw Jewish people back to Him and reconcile them with their Kinsman-Redeemer?

THE OLIVE TREE

What is presented so beautifully and poetically in Ruth, the apostle Paul presents directly, powerfully, and practically in Romans:

> I say then, **has God cast away His people? Certainly not!**...I say then, have they stumbled that they should fall? Certainly not! But **through their fall, to provoke them to jealousy, salvation has come to the Gentiles.** Now if their fall is riches for the world, and their failure

riches for the Gentiles, how much more their full-ness!....And if some of the branches were broken off, and you, being a wild olive tree, were grafted in among them, and with them became a partaker of the root and the fatness of the olive tree, do not boast against the branches. But if you do boast, remember that you do not support the root, but the root supports you. You will say then, 'Branches were broken off that I might be grafted in.' Well said. Because of unbelief they were broken off, and you stand by faith. Do not be haughty, but fear. For if God did not spare the natural branches, He may not spare you, either....And they also, if they do not continue in unbelief, will be grafted in, for God is able to graft them in again. For if you were cut out of the olive tree which is wild by nature, and were grafted contrary to nature into a cultivated olive tree, how much more will these, who are natural branches, be grafted into their own olive tree? For I do not desire, brethren, that you should be ignorant of this mystery, lest you should be wise in your own opinion, that **blindness in part has happened to Israel until the fullness of the Gentiles has come in....For the gifts and the calling of God are irrevocable.** (Romans 11:1a, 11-12, 17-21, 23-25, 29 NKJV) [Emphasis Added]

I would like to emphasize four particular themes that emerge from these verses. First, Paul establishes that God is clearly not finished with the Jewish people. Secondly, he reminds us, as Gentiles, that we are the wild branches. We are the ones who are grafted into the natural olive tree. Thirdly, Paul warns us, as Gentile Christians, against arrogance and lording our position over the Jewish people. Fourthly, he tells us that salvation has come to the Gentiles, that the Jewish people might be provoked to jealousy.

Now here is an amazing thought: **Could we, as Gentile believers, actually provoke the Jewish people to jealousy by our faith and love?** The Biblical answer, I believe, is most certainly "yes." This is a special aspect of a calling that we have in regard to the Jewish people that has been all but forgotten by the Church over the last 2,000 years. We need to remember that Jeremiah prophesied that God would make a new covenant with the house of Israel and the house of Judah (Jeremiah 31). Initially this new covenant was made with the house of Israel and the house of Judah. Jesus said very plainly, "I was sent only to the lost sheep of Israel." (Matthew 15:24) The mystery of the Gospel revealed in the New Testament is that we, as Gentiles, by the great mercy and grace of God, become partakers of the New Covenant. We become like Tamar, Rahab, and Ruth, all Gentile women who were grafted into the house of Israel and later listed in the genealogy of Jesus (Matthew 1:3, 5). We are joined to our Kinsman-Redeemer, Jesus, our "Boaz," and we become partakers of the covenant promises, just like the natural branches.

In Ephesians 2:12 Paul says that formerly the Gentiles were excluded from citizenship in Israel and foreigners to the covenants and the promises. According to Paul, the Gentiles were "far away," without hope in the world. Yet through the miracle of the Cross, God, who is rich in mercy, has drawn to Himself not just the Jewish people, but representatives from every tribe, tongue, and nation. Paul teaches that the dividing wall of hostility has been removed. The two become one — one new man in Jesus. We who were far off are brought near; we who were aliens and foreigners are now, according to Paul in Ephesians 2:19, "fellow citizens with God's people and members of God's household." Does that touch you? We were strangers, we were foreigners, we were aliens, we were without hope. But not any more. God loved Tamar, God loved Rahab, God loved Ruth; and God loves you and me as well.

So the question for us, as Gentile believers, is this: have we — as those who were once far away but have been brought near, as those who were strangers and are now citizens, as wild branches that have been grafted into the olive tree — remembered, over the last 2,000 years that God is not finished with the natural branches? Have we remembered that we are the <u>wild</u> branches...the ones that have been grafted into a Jewish olive tree, if you will, and have been connected to a Jewish Messiah? Have we remembered not to be arrogant before the Jewish people? Have we indeed, as Paul outlined, provoked the Jewish people to a holy jealousy by our faith and by our love? The next chapter will address that question in greater depth: the history of the relationship between the Church (Christianity), and the Jewish people. For now, let me simply say that **we have failed.** The Jewish people have not been provoked to jealousy by us. Instead, they have been provoked to hostility. To the Jewish people, Jesus is a "Gentile god," a Jew who abandoned and betrayed his people. Someone in whose name, and in whose sign (the cross), "Christians," and "Christian" nations, have persecuted, banished, and even murdered the Jews. As a result of historical events such as the Crusades and the Holocaust, most Jewish people want nothing to do with "Christianity." They do not have a problem so much with Jesus, *per se*, but they definitely have a problem with the legacy of the institutional Church.

THE PURITANS AND ISRAEL

Fortunately, there have been exceptions to this pattern. One notable exception was the Puritans. Many of the Puritans were "Ruths." They saw that they were a part of a "Ruth remnant" of the Church that had a calling to love and bless the Jewish people. Consider this brief excerpt from a sermon that John Owen, one of the foremost of the Puritan scholars, preached before the House of Commons in 1649:

> The Jews shall be regathered from all parts of the earth where they are scattered, and brought home into their homeland....There is not any promise anywhere of raising up a kingdom unto the Lord Jesus Christ in this world but it is either expressly, or clearly intimated, that the beginning of it must be with the Jews.[43]

A Puritan contemporary of John Owen, Robert Leighton, wrote these words:

> They forget a main point for the Church's glory who pray not daily for the conversion of the Jews. Undoubtedly, that people of the Jews shall once more be commanded to arise and shine, and their return shall be the 'riches of the Gentiles,' [Romans 11:12] and that shall be a more glorious

time than ever the Church of God did yet behold! [44]

Another Puritan leader, Samuel Rutherford, wrote many letters about his love relationship with Jesus. Charles Spurgeon said of Rutherford's letters that they were "the nearest thing to inspiration which can be found in all the writings of mere men." [45]As you read his words, *remember that this is a part of our Puritan legacy, the seed that was sown into the spiritual fabric of our nation.*

> I could stay out of heaven many years to see that victorious triumphing Lord act that prophesied part of His soul-conquering love, in taking into His kingdom the greatest sister, that kirk, [church] of the Jews....Oh, what joy and what glory would I judge it, if my heaven should be suspended till I might have leave to run on foot to be a witness of that marriage-glory, and see Christ put on the glory of His last-married bride, and His last marriage love on earth; when He shall enlarge His love-bed and set it upon the top of the mountains, and take in Elder Sister, the Jews, and the fullness of the Gentiles!...Oh to see the sight, next to Christ's Coming in the clouds, the most joyful! Our elder brethren the Jews and Christ fall upon one another's neck and kiss each other! They have been long asunder; they will be kind to one another when they meet. O day! O longed-for and lovely day – dawn! O sweet Jesus, let me see that sight which will be as life from the dead, Thee and Thy ancient people in mutual embraces. [46]

Indeed, O longed-for and lovely day — dawn!

Significantly, it is once again our Puritan fathers who show us the way. How about you? Are you willing to join them? Are you ready to rise up and join the "Ruth Remnant" of the Church?

A PRAYER IN RESPONSE

Abba, Father, we praise You that You are the great and marvelous God of Abraham, Isaac, and Jacob. You are holy and transcendent, yet in mercy You have stooped down to earth through

Your Son, Jesus, Y'shua. You have provided for the salvation of Your Jewish people. You have provided for the salvation of the Gentiles. Thank You, Abba, for the mystery of the Gospel — the "one new man," with the wall of hostility removed; Jew and Gentile, together, expressing the glory of God and the beauty of the Gospel. I pray that believers all over this nation would have ears to hear and eyes to see the significance of what You are doing in this generation among unreached Gentile peoples, and among Your chosen Jewish people. O, Lord, that we would be like Ruth! O Father, raise us up as "Ruths" who would say to Jewish people, "Your God is our God." Grant that we would bind our hearts to theirs — to love them, to nourish them, and to bless them. Grant that we would not forsake "Naomi," as did Orpah, but that we would cling to her as "Ruths." Abba, give the Gentile Church a fresh understanding of that aspect of her calling that has been long forgotten: to love and bless the Jewish people. Would You so use us to love and nourish the Jewish people, that they would be restored to their Messiah. As Ruth loved Naomi, so may we love Your chosen people. We pray, Abba, for revival among the Gentiles. We also pray for revival among the Jewish people — for their physical and their spiritual restoration — all for Your great glory. In Jesus' name, Amen.

CHAPTER NINE

The History of the Church and the Jewish People: A Bitter Legacy

efore the Church of Jesus Christ today lies a momentous opportunity to bless the Jewish people and to love them into loving Jesus — Y'shua. As I shared in the last chapter, I truly believe the Lord is calling forth a "Ruth remnant" from the Church. But in order to be a part of what our God is doing — and is about to do — it is imperative that we as Gentile Christians have a better understanding of the history of the relationship between the Church and the Jewish people. Without this understanding we will never be able to identify with the tremendous pain that Jewish people feel as they remember this history. We will never be able to grasp the misconceptions Jewish people have about Jesus and about true Biblical Christian faith. And, as a result, we will never be able to be used redemptively and restoratively in the lives of Jewish people.

A brief historical survey is important, therefore, so that we may approach our calling as "Ruths" with greater wisdom and sensitivity. Unfortunately, for the most part, this history has not been characterized by the attitude of our Puritan forebears in England and the United States. It is a history that you may find difficult to read, even to believe. May the Lord give us open minds and hearts. Indeed, may the Lord grant us His heart.

THE EARLY CHURCH AND THE JEWS

After the apostolic era ended and as more and more non-Jews became Christians, the body of Christ became increasingly Gentile. As such, it also became easier for the Gentiles, being in the overwhelming majority, to arrogantly lord their position over the Jewish people, even though the Apostle Paul had warned very clearly against such an attitude in Romans, chapters 9-11. It is a sad fact that by the middle of the third century AD, most Christians believed that the destruction of Jerusalem in 70 AD and the accompanying dispersion of the Jews at that time were God's way of showing the Jewish people that He was finished with them. In fact, one of our early church fathers, Origen, wrote in his book, <u>Against Celsus</u>, that the Jews "will never be restored to their former condition. For they have committed a crime of the most unhallowed kind, in conspiring against the Saviour of the human race." [47]

CONSTANTINE AND THE JEWS

In 306 AD, a church decree was issued in Elvira, Spain that forbade Christians to receive blessings from Jewish people. At the Nicene Councils called in 325 AD and 787 AD, Jewish leaders were not even invited to participate.[48] The Emperor Constantine called the Nicene council of 325 primarily to address doctrinal problems, but he also wanted to make sure that the Church separated herself from the Jewish people, those "polluted wretches" who had stained their hands with "a nefarious crime." Constantine wanted a date for the celebration of the Resurrection other than Passover, because it was too Jewish. To the bishops assembled in Nicea he wrote: "It appeared an unworthy thing that in the celebration of this most holy feast, we should follow the practice of the Jews, who have impiously defiled their hands with an enormous sin, and are, therefore, deservedly afflicted with blindness of soul." [49]

What about what the Apostle Paul had written in Romans 11:1, "Did God reject his people? By no means!" Or in Romans 11:11, "Did they stumble so as to fall beyond recovery? Not at all!" What about Jeremiah's prophecy that Israel would be a nation as long as the sun shines by day and the moon and stars by night? (Jeremiah 31:35-37)

Constantine did have his way, however. Worship on the Sabbath was banned, and the Biblical Jewish feasts were replaced with Christianized pagan ones. For example, the annual celebration of the Lord's Resurrection would now be called Easter, which bears a striking similarity to Eostre, the Teutonic goddess of spring. Also at this time, Jews who had come to faith in Christ were now expected to completely sever any connection to their Jewish heritage. If they refused, these "heretics" fell under the wrath of an increasingly confused Gentile church. As a result of the second Nicean council in 787, believing Jews had to prove to the Church that they were indeed "Christians." Tragically, the council issued a decree that excluded Jews from communion unless they renounced the observance of the Sabbath, or any other of their other Jewish customs.

The Lateran Councils of `1179 AD and 1215 AD initiated an ominous trend. Jews were ordered to live in separate parts of the city, and to wear distinctive dress. Does that sound familiar? Such a church policy ultimately helped prepare the way for Jewish "ghetto" living throughout Europe, and even the wearing of yellow badges both before and during the Nazi era.[50]

Another of our church fathers, John Chrysostom, gave eight "Homilies against the Jews" in the late 3ʳᵈ and early 4ᵗʰ centuries. Chrysostom, whose very name means "golden mouthed," was known as one of the most eloquent preachers of truth and love. To this day he is esteemed as one of the greatest of our church fathers.[51] Here is what he had to say about the Jewish people:

> The synagogue is worse than a brothel...it is a den of scoundrels and the repair of wild beasts...the temple of demons devoted to idolatrous cults...the refuge of brigands and debauchees, and the cavern of devils. [It is] a criminal assembly of Jews...a place of meeting for the assassins of Christ...a house worse than a drinking shop...a den of thieves; a house of ill fame, a dwelling of iniquity, the refuge of devils, a gulf and abyss of perdition....As for me,

I hate the synagogue....I hate the Jews for the same reason.[52]

As if that were not bad enough, in another sermon John Chrysostom also wrote,

> They sacrificed their sons and daughters to devils: they outraged nature and overthrew from their foundations the laws of relationships. They are become worse than wild beasts, and for no reason at all, with their own hands they murder their offspring, to worship the avenging devils who are the foes of our life...they are lustful, rapacious, greedy, perfidious bandits...inveterate murderers, destroyers, men possessed by the devil...debauchery, drunkenness have given them the manners of a pig and the lusty goat. They know only one thing, to satisfy their gullets, get drunk, to kill and maim one another. (Chrysostom's sermons as quoted by Parkes, *'The Conflict of the Church and Synagogue'*, pp.163-164) [53]

Bernard of Clairvaux, one of the most influential Christian monks of the Middle Ages, imputed to the Jewish people "a stupidity, bestial and more than bestial." He called them an "evil seed" and "a race who had not God for their father, but were of the devil, and were murderers as he was a murderer from the beginning." [54]

THE THEOLOGICAL ROOT OF ANTI-SEMITISM: "REPLACEMENT THEOLOGY"

It is almost impossible to believe that respected early church fathers said and wrote such things. I want to stress that I am not condemning these men, many of whom were used of God in a mighty way. Yet, at the same time, how could they believe and propagate such lies? I believe the answer lies in a deception that slowly crept into the church, an errant teaching known as Replacement Theology. According to Replacement Theology, the Jewish people have lost their status as the "chosen people" because they rejected Jesus as the Messiah. Instead, the Church has replaced them in God's plans, inheriting the promises originally intended for Israel. On this flawed foundation, so-called Christian anti-Semitism easily crept into the Church and its practices, even at times resulting in persecution of the Jewish people. Today, we, as Christians, need to be aware of this deception and the enduring pain it has caused the Jewish people. We need to be educated, and to educate other Christians as well, so that we might renounce this aspect of the legacy of the Church. Then, we will be able to relate to the Jewish people with a true understanding of what the Bible says about their past, their present, and their future.

THE CRUSADES

From the 11th to the 13th Centuries, the Church launched several Crusades aimed at liberating the Holy Land from the Muslims. During the Crusader era the slogan was born, "Kill a Jew and save your soul." [55] Each time these Crusades were launched, large fanatical armies marched through Europe, and what would become modern Turkey, to the Holy Land. Along the way the Crusaders would persecute not only Jewish people, but Eastern Christians, and Muslims as well.

Pope Urban II issued the call to the First Crusade in 1095 in Cologne, Germany. In 1096 the Crusaders began a three-year trek across Europe and the Middle East. Pillaging and plundering as they went, the Crusaders reached the Holy Land in the summer of 1099. Finally on July 15th, 1099, the Crusaders conquered Jerusalem. The Jewish inhabitants of the city, hoping to be spared, sought refuge in the chief synagogue. But, their hope was in vain. The Crusaders surrounded the synagogue and set it ablaze. They raised high their Crusader crosses and sang "Christ We Adore Thee," while they watched their helpless Jewish captives suffer an agonizing death. One of the leaders of the Crusaders, Raymond of Aguiller, commenting on the horrible events that day, quoted Psalm 118:24: "This is the day the Lord has made; let us rejoice and be glad in it." [56]

Is it any wonder that for Jewish people, the sign of the Cross, or even the name "Christian," evokes a visceral reaction of fear and resentment? To us, the words "cross" and "Christian" hold sacred meanings; but to the Jews, they are symbols of persecution. I am sure that most readers of this book are not even familiar with this history. I did not know it myself until a few years ago, but I assure you that it is uppermost in the minds, hearts, and souls of the Jewish people. If we do not understand the impact of this history, then we can very easily and unknowingly short-circuit our testimony. Thinking we are drawing Jewish people to the Messiah, we may very well drive them away instead, through words and actions that are insensitive and completely misperceived.

THE MIDDLE AGES

In 1348 and 1349, the Black Death swept through Europe, annihilating about one third of the total population. Who was scapegoated for this terrible pestilence? The Jewish people. The fact that multitudes of Jewish people also died as victims of the plague did not seem to matter. The Jewish people were blamed for secretly contaminating wells with a poisonous mixture of spiders, lizards, and the hearts of Christians mixed together with the elements of the Eucharist. Many Christians believed this false charge, and as a result, thousands of Jews were massacred by furious mobs.[57]

Two other charges made against the Jewish people in the Middle Ages were "the desecration of the host" and ritual murder. I will explain "desecration of the host" first. According to the Roman Catholic doctrine of transubstantiation, the communion wafer and the wine actually become the body and blood of Jesus. It is believed that the partaker actually does eat the body and drink the blood of Jesus. Once officially adopted by the church in 1215, this doctrine of transubstantiation opened the door for another charge against the Jewish people. It was asserted that having crucified Jesus once, they would of course want to crucify Him over and over again. Throughout the Middle Ages Jews would often be accused of stealing, torturing, and killing Jesus by torturing these communion wafers which, of course, were considered to be the very body of Christ. In 1243, Berlin's entire Jewish population was burned alive for allegedly desecrating the host. Similar persecutions took place against the Jewish communities in Prague in 1389, and in Berlin in 1510. A charge of desecration of the host was even leveled as recently as 1836 in Romania.[58]

A second charge commonly brought against the Jews of the Middle Ages was that of ritual murder. Jews would allegedly kidnap Christian children, usually before Easter, torturing and killing them, often by crucifixion. They would then, so the charge goes, drink some of the blood and then use the rest to prepare their Passover matzo. The fact that there was no evidence — other than confessions of Jewish people who had been tortured — made no difference. How many Jewish people lost their lives at the hands of the institutional "Church" and so-called Christians because of such fallacious charges, we do not know; but the number was certainly in the many tens of thousands.[59]

THE INQUISITIONS

Church inquisitions took place throughout Central and Western Europe from the 12ᵗʰ to the 19ᵗʰ centuries. The most notorious and well-known occurred in Spain. The Jews were not the only victims of the Spanish Inquisition, but certainly they were among them. Jews who had converted to Catholicism and been baptized were called Marranos. Despite their conversion to Christianity, the Marranos were viewed with deep suspicion by the Roman Catholic Church. If they engaged in any so-called heretical practices — keeping a kosher kitchen, observing the Sabbath, or celebrating the Biblical feasts — they could be persecuted, exiled, or even burned at the stake. Incredibly, approximately 30,000 Marranos were burned at the stake during the Spanish Inquisitions. And as if that were not enough, all non-baptized Jews were then forcibly expelled from Spain in 1492. Similar expulsions also took place in England as well as many other European countries during the Middle Ages.[60]

MARTIN LUTHER AND THE JEWS

Protestant Christians regard the Reformation as one of the bright spots of church history. Protestants applaud the return to such Biblical doctrines as salvation by faith (*sola fide*), salvation by grace (*sola gracia*), and the ultimate authority of the Scriptures (*sola scriptura*). Martin Luther is remembered with respect and esteem throughout the Christian world as the courageous initiator of the Protestant Reformation.

Interestingly enough, when Luther began the Reformation, he also broke with the prevailing attitude of the Roman Catholic Church toward the Jewish people. Early in the Reformation, Luther wrote:

> Perhaps I will attract some of the Jews to the Christian faith. For our fools — the popes, bishops, sophists, and monks — the coarse blockheads! have until this time so treated the Jews that...if I had been a Jew, and had seen such idiots and block-heads ruling and teaching the Christian religion, I would rather have been a sow than a Christian. For they have dealt with the Jews as if they were dogs and not human beings.[61] (Brown, p. 14)

Unfortunately, by the end of his life, Martin Luther had changed his position 180 degrees, writing venomous things against the Jewish people. When I first learned of this, I was confused by this adamant reversal. "How could Martin Luther, this man so mightily used of God, turn against the Jewish people?" I believe the Lord showed me that the answer lies in a combination of woundedness in his life, sin, and very intense spiritual warfare.

By contemporary standards, Martin Luther was most certainly abused by his father. He later said that his chief struggle in regard to sin was anger. I believe that as Martin Luther began to reach out to the Jewish people and was rebuffed, he was hurt and wounded. The hurt then became bitterness and resentment. These attitudes then provided a stronghold or platform from which the enemy could operate in his life. In saying all this, do I condemn Martin Luther? No, I do not. I am so thankful for his impact on the Church in many ways. At the same time, we also need to face the ugly truth about this aspect of Martin Luther's legacy. Sadly, this is what Luther wrote twenty years after the start of the Reformation:

> What shall we Christians do with this damned, rejected race of Jews? First, their synagogues should be set on fire....Secondly, their homes should likewise be broken down and destroyed....Thirdly, they should be deprived of their prayer-books and Talmuds....Fourthly, their rabbis

must be forbidden under threat of death to teach any more....Fifthly, passport and traveling privileges should be absolutely forbidden to the Jews....Sixthly, they ought to be stopped from usury [charging excessive interest on loans]....Seventhly, let the young and strong Jews and Jewesses be given the flail, the axe, the hoe, the spade, the distaff, and spindle, and let them earn their bread by the sweat of their noses....We ought to drive their rascally lazy bones out of our system....Therefore away with them....

To sum up, dear princes and nobles who have Jews in your domains, if this advice of mine does not suit you, then find a better one so that you and we may all be free of this insufferable devilish burden — the Jews.[62]

On another occasion Luther wrote:

Burn their synagogues and schools; what will not burn, bury with earth, that neither stone nor rubbish remain. In like manner break into and destroy their homes. Take away their prayer books and Talmuds, in which there is nothing but godlessness, lies, cursing and swearing. Forbid their rabbis to teach, on pain of life or limb....If I had power over them I would assemble their most prominent men and demand that they prove we Christians do not worship God, under penalty of having their tongues torn out through the back of the neck. (Stevens 'Strife Between Brothers', Olive Press, St. Albans: 1979, p. 34)[63]

In 20ᵗʰ-century Germany, Adolph Hitler did not have to look very far to find justification for his hatred of the Jews. Martin Luther is quoted in this demonized murderer's work, *Mein Kampf.*

During the twelve years of the Thousand Year Reich, "Christian" Germany, a nation at that time about half Catholic and half Lutheran, stood idly by while their Fuhrer systematically murdered 6,000,000 Jews.

THE 20TH CENTURY

The Jews of Europe endured persecution and forced exile in the "pogroms" of Poland and Russia in the 19th and 20th centuries. These pogroms took place in "Christian" countries in which there was an alliance between the Church and the state. During this period the motto of the fanatical masses became, "Beat the Jews and save Russia." [64] Even today we see a rebirth of vehement anti-Semitism in Russia. In 1998, just before my family left Russia to move to Israel, I saw written on the wall of a St. Petersburg train station, "Beat the Jews — save Russia."

The most horrific aspect of this history of the relationship between the Church and the Jewish people is the Holocaust. We are much more familiar with the Holocaust than with many of these other events. Therefore, I will not spend a lot of time on it, other than to note once again that six million Jewish people in the heart of European "Christendom" — nations with established state churches and many professing Christians — were enslaved, starved, gassed, and burned, for no other reason than that they were Jewish. In most of these nations, Christians did either very little or nothing at all to resist, or to seek to save the Jewish people. Certainly there were exceptions among the so-called "righteous Gentiles" such as Corrie ten Boom and Raoul Wallenberg, but unfortunately, the masses did nothing. The Jews were trapped and murdered like animals.

Addressing what made the "final solution" possible, Holocaust scholar Raoul Hillberg wrote:

> Since the fourth century after Christ, there have been three anti-Jewish policies: [forced] conversion, expulsion, and annihilation. The second appeared as an alternative to the first, and the third emerged as an alternative to the second....The missionaries of Christianity had said in effect: You have no right to live among us as Jews. [Meaning that the Jews had to live as Gentiles and could not live a Jewish life or maintain their Jewish customs.] The secular rulers who followed proclaimed: You have no right to live among us. The Nazis at last decreed: You have no right to live....The German Nazis, then, did not discard

the past; they built upon it. They did not begin a development; they completed it.[65]

I realize that for many of you this may be a very difficult history to read. It may seem to be literally unbelievable. You may be in shock, as I was when I first heard it a few years ago. I grew up in a Christian home and was taught by my parents to love the Jewish people. I had many Jewish friends. As a young tennis player, my first doubles partner was an Orthodox Jew. I grew up in a church that taught the special role of the Jewish people in God's plans. I had never heard of "Replacement Theology," and I did not know any of this history until relatively recently. Yet we, as Christians, need to know it. We need to know the truth, so that we can understand the chasm that exists between the Jewish people and true Biblical Christianity, because of this horrible legacy bequeathed to us. Indeed, we have not provoked the Jews to jealousy; instead, we have provoked them to hostility, bitterness, and resentment. In so doing, we and our fathers have sinned.

HOW SHOULD WE RESPOND?

So what can you and I do? How do we respond? When I first learned about this history, I was mortified and deeply grieved. Out of this grief the Holy Spirit birthed in me a strong desire to be a reconciler. Christians are called to be ambassadors of reconciliation in regard to the gospel. Yet if we want to love the Jewish people into loving Y'shua, we first need to be reconcilers in regard to the deep wounds still present in the collective Jewish soul, *vis à vis* Christianity and the Church. I assure you that every Jewish person knows this history that you may be reading about for the first time today. Indeed, a collective sense of woundedness, as well as a reservoir of grief and distrust, exists deep in the Jewish soul. I also believe, however, that the Lord can begin to heal this wound through Gentile believers who are willing to be reconcilers.

I wrote earlier in this chapter about the horrible atrocities that accompanied the first Crusade. Now I would like to tell you about a Christian initiative that took place a few years ago, to repent for the first Crusade. The "Reconciliation Walk" was an interdenominational effort to walk the route of the first Crusade, with the participants repenting, confessing sin, and asking forgiveness of Eastern Christians, Muslims, and Jews, all along the way. As the first Crusade was initiated in Cologne in 1095, so 900 years later, in 1995, Christians gathered there in a spirit of humility and repentance. Then, many Christians joined the walk for whatever period of time they could, journeying across Europe to the Middle East, for three years, from 1996 to 1999.

Having moved to Israel in the summer of 1999, I was privileged to participate in the final week of the Reconciliation Walk in Jerusalem. Participants attended official ceremonies in which Western Christians repented before the chief rabbis of Israel. We also walked the streets and approached Jewish people, presenting a written apology and telling them how sorry we were for what "Christians" had done. We told them that this was not the true spirit of Christianity or of Y'shua (Jesus). We explained that this history grieved Him, and that it grieved us as well. We were coming simply to repent, ask forgiveness, and show the true love of Y'shua (Jesus).

I will never forget one conversation I had with a shopkeeper in the Jewish quarter of the Old City. As we shared the apology with her and asked her forgiveness, she replied, "Of course I will forgive you! I know that this is not who Jesus is, or what Jesus taught. In fact," she said, "what you are doing is a beautiful thing. You are wonderful people. It's people like you who are going to come and bring — oh, I don't know the word in English, but in Hebrew, the word is *yeshuáh*."

Yeshuáh [yeh-shoo-AH] means **salvation**. *Y'shúa* [yeh-SHOO-uh] is the name for **Jesus**. I was astounded by the significance of her words. I believe this unbelieving Jewish woman was speaking prophetically though she did not even know it. She was saying that Gentile believers, coming in the true spirit of Jesus, would be the ones who could come as true agents of reconciliation and bring, yes, salvation (yeshuáh) through Y'shúa (Jesus). It is that type of Christian who will be able to be used of the Lord, not only to soften the hearts of Jewish people, but also, like Ruth, to introduce them to their Kinsman-Redeemer.

BECOMING RECONCILERS

So how do we respond to this history? How do we begin to become reconcilers? I would like to suggest five responses that I believe would be both pleasing to the Lord and eternally significant as well.

1. We can enter into identificational repentance in a way similar to Daniel (Dan. 9:1-19), Ezra (Ezra 9:6-7), and Nehemiah (Neh. 1:6-7). We can confess the sins of the institutional church and of our forefathers against the Jewish people. The Reconciliation Walk is a formal example of this, but we can also do the same thing in relationships with Jewish people whom the Lord puts in our paths.

2. We can give ourselves to prayer and fasting, interceding for reconciliation between Jew and Gentile in the Body of Christ, and for the salvation of the Jewish people. I have a dream that in the generation ahead we will see the emergence of a true, "one new man" expression of the Body of Christ (Ephesians chapter 2). Jews and Gentiles, embracing one another, understanding one another, accepting one another, affording each other the freedom to be Jewish or to be Gentile. Gentiles can to continue to practice their Gentile Christian traditions, while Jewish people are free to celebrate the Feasts and other Jewish customs.

3. Perhaps some Gentile believers will also desire to celebrate the feasts. My family does, and we love it! For us as Gentiles, it is as though we have been cut off from our Jewish roots in a way that is unhealthy. When the Nicean Council selected a different date for the celebration of the Resurrection of Jesus, the Church was cut off from a Biblical Passover celebration. It is my conviction that when we as Christians understand the Old Testament feasts, then the fulfillment that came through Jesus becomes that much more meaningful. For example, do you realize that the spring feasts — Passover, the Feast of Unleavened Bread, the Feast of First Fruits, and the Feast of Weeks (Pentecost) — were all prophetic? They all pointed to the first coming of Y'shua, Jesus. They were all fulfilled literally in His first coming. When my family and I celebrate them, we are remembering the fulfillment that came through Jesus.

Celebrating the Biblical feasts also opens up opportunities to witness to Jewish people, because we can say, "Yes, we're Gentiles, but we celebrate these Biblical feasts." As we have an opportunity to get to know them, we can first hear about their traditions, but then share what we believe as well. The fall feasts — the Feast of Trumpets, the Day of Atonement, and the Feast of Tabernacles — will all be fulfilled at Jesus' Second Coming. We can now celebrate those feasts, looking forward to, praying for, and hoping for the coming of our blessed Savior.

I believe that it is God's heart to bring forth a "one new man" expression of the Body of Christ that is even greater than that of the first century. Scripture tells us that Jesus sent the disciples out in twos to preach the Good News. Imagine witnessing teams going out to the nations in twos — a Jew and a Gentile. The Jewish person will testify, "My people have rejected the Messiah for 2,000 years, but I'm here to say 'Y'shua is my Messiah! Y'shua is the Messiah of the Jewish people, and yet He's your Messiah, too.'" Imagine the Gentile then proclaiming, "Yes, I agree with my Jewish brother — He's the Messiah for the Jews, but He's our Messiah, too. We are one, Jew and Greek, in Jesus — Y'shua — the Christ, the Messiah." Consider the awesome potential for harvest! Imagine the anointing with which the Lord would grace such a "one new man" testimony to the nations! I encourage you to pray for that day. Pray for such a one new man testimony to arise, and ask the Lord to anoint it with such power that there would indeed be a great harvest among the nations.

4. We can ask the Lord to make us like the Sons of Issachar so that we would understand His heart for the Church and the Jewish people in our day. We can ask Him to use us personally in His purposes for reconciliation and harvest.

5. We can learn to present the gospel wisely, sensitively, and lovingly to the Jewish people. We can distinguish between the true nature of Jesus and His teachings, and "Christianity" and the institutional church as the Jewish people see them. When a Jewish person asks me if I am a Christian, the answer I give might surprise you — even shock you. **I typically reply, "No, I'm not a Christian — <u>not as you understand it</u>."** Such an answer mystifies them, and gives me an opportunity to share in a nutshell the message of this chapter. I tell Jewish people about the deception of Replacement Theology that crept into the Church, and then contrast

that with the true calling that we have to love and bless the Jewish people. I distance myself from Christian anti-Semitism and all the things that have been done in the name of Jesus and in the sign of the cross. I share that such events are not at all reflective of the true spirit of Christianity or the teaching of Jesus. In this way, I have a chance to disarm the visceral reaction against Biblical Christian faith, and, I hope, lovingly mystify the Jewish people in a way that can provoke a godly jealousy. I desire to communicate that I am a "different" kind of Gentile, who loves the Jews, who loves the *Tanakh* (the Old Testament), who loves the Biblical feasts, who loves the Jewish Messiah, and who relates to the Jewish people in a different way.

We cannot witness to Jewish people <u>in the exact same manner</u> as we witness to others. Yes, the Jewish people need to be saved, as any other people. But if we use the same terminology, the same lingo, and approach them in the same way, as we would to others who don't have the excess baggage of this history, then we are making a big mistake. Thinking we are loving them, we could be actually driving them farther away from the Lord.

6. We can bless the Jewish people in several concrete ways. First of all, we can ask the Lord to purify us of any form of anti-Semitism that may be lurking in our hearts: Anti-Semitic jokes, anti-Semitic attitudes, or even a bitterness or resentment against Jewish people. We need to ask the Lord to search our hearts. If He reveals any of the above, we can confess it, ask forgiveness, renounce it, and then ask the Lord to give us instead a love for the Jewish people.

Secondly, we can bless the Jewish people by looking for concrete ways to encourage, love, and minister to those in our circles of influence, whether they are ready to accept the Messiah or not. Do not reject Jewish people if they are hostile toward your presentation of Y'shua/Jesus as the Messiah. Love them! Remember the testimony of Ruth. Bind your heart to them, and be willing to lovingly and patiently reconnect them with their Kinsman-Redeemer.

Thirdly, we can bless the Jewish people by praying for and supporting financially the return of new immigrants to Israel. Many organizations facilitate *"aliyah,"* that is, the return and repatriation of Jews to their homeland.[66] Other organizations specialize in reaching Jewish people with the gospel.

Fourthly, we can commit to pray daily for Israel and the Jewish people. I challenge you to ask the Lord if He is calling you to pray daily for the Jewish people. Pray for their salvation. Pray for that day when the veil will be completely removed and the Jewish people will look upon Him whom they have pierced, and embrace their Messiah through many tears.

Beloved, we have a glorious calling, not only as ambassadors of reconciliation to the nations, but also as ambassadors of reconciliation to the Jewish people. I want to be a reconciler, and I pray the Lord would make us reconcilers, so that we can be a part of the fulfillment of His purposes as He draws more and more Jewish people to Himself in our day. Remember, more Jews have come to the Messiah since 1967 than from the 4th century to that time. Praise the Lord for the awesome work He is doing in the hearts of Jews and Gentiles. Our God is on the move!

A PRAYER IN RESPONSE

Father in heaven, the history that we have read today is difficult to hear. We're shocked and appalled; we're grieved, and we almost cannot believe that it is true. Yet, it is true. Father, as we hear it, we are ashamed and deeply distressed that things like this were done by the Church, by professing Christians under the sign of the cross and in the name of Jesus. O Father, we confess these sins against the Jewish people. We identify with the sins of our forefathers, and we ask for Your forgiveness. We pray that You would use us to take the sting out of this wound that exists in the hearts and souls of Jewish people. We pray that You would make us true reconcilers, first in regard to these wounds, and then in regard to the Gospel of Y'shua, the Messiah. We ask You to indeed bring reconciliation in the Body between Jew and Gentile. We pray for a day in which Jews and Gentiles would go together in unity and preach the Gospel, to the Jew first, and then to the Gentile. Anoint such a testimony and bring forth an unprecedented harvest among the nations. Father, I pray that You would use us to bless Jewish people. Teach us to bless Jewish people so meaningfully and so powerfully that they would be both mystified and provoked to jealousy. A godly jealousy that would lead them to brokenness, humility, repentance, and faith in their Messiah. We pray it for their sake, and for the sake of Y'shua, who longs for their embrace. Amen.

CHAPTER TEN

Blessing or Cursing?

**"I will bless those who bless you,
and whoever curses you I will curse."
Genesis 12:3**

What a powerful declaration of God's intent! Did God really mean it? Does the above Scripture have any relevance for us today? Would God actually bless an individual or nation for blessing the Jews, or curse them for in some way cursing the Jews? Was such a promise valid only in Biblical history, or perhaps up until the beginning of the Great Diaspora in 70 AD? Or, has this promise been valid from the day God gave it until now? If this promise is true, the ramifications are powerful indeed for the nations of the earth, and for the Church of Jesus Christ in those nations.

If the promise of Genesis 12:3 is indeed true, then we would expect to find evidence both in Biblical history, and in events taking place since that time as well. Does such evidence exist? Are there indeed historical examples that testify to the stated truth of Genesis 12:3? If so, the United States and, for that matter, all the nations of the earth, should tremble before God as they make decisions relating to Israel, or the land of Israel, and the Jewish people dispersed throughout the world.

My purpose in this chapter is not to provide an in-depth historical examination in order to "prove" the truth of Genesis 12:3. Indeed, a whole book could be devoted to this topic. My goal is to stimulate prayerful research of history past, as well as watchful analysis of current events. For many years, I have believed this "thesis" to be true. I hope to whet your appetite and stir your further consideration through the presentation of many historical examples. The bottom line, I believe, is that God does indeed act in history according to the promise He made to Abraham in Genesis 12:3.

EGYPT AND BABYLON

No sooner had God made this promise to Abraham, than He afflicted the Egyptian Pharoah with a serious disease after he had taken Sarai into his palace (Genesis 12:17). According to Genesis 20, Abimelech suffered similar consequences for the same offense, but was later blessed when Abraham interceded for him (20:17-18).

God certainly blessed the kingdom of Egypt as Pharoah blessed Joseph, making him the second-in-command of all Egypt. In contrast, Egypt suffered horrible consequences for her later oppression of the Hebrews. Much later, the Lord raised up Babylonia to discipline Judah for her sins, but then judged Babylonia for her harsh treatment of the Jews. "Before your eyes I will repay Babylon and all who live in Babylonia for all the wrong they have done in Zion" (Jeremiah 51:24).[67]

THE ROMAN EMPIRE

Is it merely by chance that not 50 years after Constantine initiated his anti-Semitic laws that the Roman Empire split in two in AD 364? [68]

SPAIN

Spain was the most powerful nation in 15th-century Europe. At the pinnacle of her power, Spain launched the Spanish Inquisition, and then in 1492 expelled 300,000 Jews. Spain's dominance on the world stage declined rapidly. Within 100 years, the British navy crushed the Spanish Armada in 1588. Spain never fully recovered.[69]

MARTIN LUTHER

In 1546, Martin Luther preached his most hateful sermon against the Jews, one that Adolph Hitler would later claim as "Christian" justification for his plans to annihilate European Jewry. Within a week, Martin Luther, the great Reformer, was dead.[70]

RUSSIA

Perhaps no nation has been more consistently anti-Semitic than Russia. In the late 19th and early 20th centuries, Jews suffered horribly during the "Pogroms." Thousands were killed and many more fled the country in great terror. Is it a coincidence that within 20 years of the Pogroms, the glory of Russia disappeared, replaced by the 70-year-long nightmare of Communism?

GREAT BRITAIN

In 1917, Great Britain promised a homeland for the Jewish people in the "Balfour Declaration." At the end of World War I, Great Britain stood at the pinnacle of her power. "The sun never sets on the British Empire," it was said. Soon, however, Great Britain began to renege on her promise to the Jews. In 1922 she ceded 76% of the territory promised to the Jews, to Trans Jordan. That very year, the troubles in Ireland erupted into a firestorm that has been a thorn in the side of Great Britain ever since.

In the 1920s and 1930s, Great Britain began to restrict Jewish immigration to Palestine, in order to curry the favor of the Arabs in the Middle East. Even during World War II, the British refused to open up Palestine to the flood of suffering Jews trying desperately to escape the jaws of the "final solution." Six million Jewish men, women, and children were trapped in Europe with no place to go.

Is it mere chance that Great Britain never fully recovered from World War II? Her empire disappeared virtually without a fight, and within a generation Great Britain became another second-rate European power.[71]

GERMANY

Germany, under the leadership of Adolph Hitler, perpetrated unspeakable horrors against the Jewish people. Within just a few years, more than 6,000,000 Jews perished in the Holocaust. Is it a coincidence that as a result, Germany was so severely crushed at the end of the war, even suffering the humiliation of being divided in half? Yet, after the war, following the payment of a large sum of reparations to the Jews, West Germany emerged as an economic powerhouse in the new post-war Europe.[72]

THE UNITED STATES OF AMERICA

The United States has been a haven for the world's Jews for hundreds of years. American Jews have been welcomed and have prospered here like nowhere else. For the most part, they have dwelt in security without fear. The United States was the first nation to recognize the infant state of Israel, just minutes after David Ben Gurion proclaimed the birth of the modern State of Israel. Since World War II, America has enjoyed unprecedented prosperity and power. At the turn of the 21ˢᵗ Century, she stands alone as the world's sole superpower.

Yet, could it be that storm clouds are gathering on the horizon of America's future? Israel has had no greater friend than the United States. Israel trusts America as she has trusted no other ally. America stands in a position to bless Israel as she has never been blessed, or to curse her perhaps through an unwitting betrayal. Since the end of the Gulf War, the U.S. has supported the premise of "Land for Peace" in an effort to resolve the crisis in the Middle East and secure the world's oil supply. Presidents George H.W. Bush, Bill Clinton, and George W. Bush have all put pressure on Israel to give up a portion of her covenant land, in return for Arab guarantees of peace. Even now, George W. Bush is the prime mover behind the so-called "Road Map for Peace." If he is successful, Israel will suffer the consequence of being left with virtually indefensible borders. If the U.S. is responsible for compromising the security of our best friend in the Middle East, the "Road Map for Peace" may in fact become the "Road Map for Disaster" for the United States.

IS GOD WARNING AMERICA?

If Genesis 12:3 is indeed true, then it would apply to the United States' relationship with Israel as well. If we have indeed been courting danger through the "Land for Peace" campaign, we would expect that the Lord would seek to warn us to turn from this present course. Have we received such warnings since the end of the Gulf War? **Has the Lord been trying to tell us something?**

It is imperative that we as Americans — and particularly American Christians — learn from the lessons of history. It is equally imperative that we learn to recognize what is happening before our very eyes. If the Lord is speaking a prophetic message to us through current events, we would do well to discern His counsel and heed it.

Authors John McTernan and Bill Koenig have done extensive media research, seeking to determine if American's pro-land-give-away policies have resulted in warnings and/or judgments from God. Their thesis is that each time the U.S. makes a public pronouncement at odds with Israel's Biblical right to her covenant land, God quickly responds with a corrective word of warning. McTernan and Koenig present many examples in their book, Israel: The Blessing or the Curse. For our purposes here, I will mention just a few such instances, from the presidencies of George H.W. Bush, Bill Clinton, and George W. Bush.

October 30-31, 1991

On October 30, 1991, President George H.W. Bush sponsored the Madrid Middle East Peace Conference. This conference marked the beginning of the "Land for Peace" process. Also on October 30th, the now-famous "Perfect Storm" arose in the North Atlantic Ocean. On October 31, this incredibly powerful storm slammed into New England. Waves as high as 30 feet pounded President Bush's vacation home in Kennebunkport, Maine, causing extensive damage. President Bush had to adjust his travel schedule in order to go inspect the damage.[73]

August 23, 1992

The Madrid Peace Conference reconvened in Washington, DC on August 23, 1992. The very same day, Hurricane Andrew, the worst natural disaster in American history, blasted into southern Florida. Damage estimates ran as high as $30 billion.[74]

January 16, 1994

President Clinton met in Geneva with Syria's president, Hafez el-Assad, to discuss peace negotiations between Israel and Syria. Syria demanded return of the strategic Golan Heights as a precondition for peace. According to American newspapers, Clinton said, "Israel must make concessions that will be politically unpopular with many Israelis." Within 24 hours, a 6.9-magnitude earthquake devastated Northridge, California. The quake was the second-most destructive natural disaster in American history.[75]

January 21, 1998

Israeli Prime Minister Benjamin Netanyahu visited the U.S. for talks with President Clinton and Secretary of State Madeline Albright. Both leaders put tremendous pressure on Netanyahu to make concessions to the Palestinians. Netanyahu was given a chilly welcome — the President and the Secretary of State refused to even have lunch with the Prime Minister. Not long after the end of their meeting, the infamous Clinton/Lewinsky sex scandal broke and became headline news.[76]

May 3, 1999

On May 3, 1999, the most powerful tornadoes in American history struck Oklahoma and Texas. They hit on the same day (May 4, Israeli time) that Yasser Arafat intended to proclaim a Palestinian State, with its capital in Jerusalem. President Clinton persuaded Arafat to postpone such a declaration, but he wrote Arafat a letter, supporting the Palestinians' right to "determine their own future in their own land." [77]

May 22, 2001

President George W. Bush and Secretary of State Colin Powell both publicly announced their support of the Mitchell Report. This official document recommended a series of steps toward the ultimate goal of Israel giving land to the Palestinians, in exchange for promises of peace. At the same time as the President's declarations of support, rumors began flying that the U.S. Senator from Vermont, James Jeffords, was planning to leave the Republican Party. On May 25, President Bush nominated Daniel Kurtzner as the new U.S. Ambassador to Israel. It was Kurzner who, as a speechwriter for former Secretary of State James Baker, first used the phrase "land for peace." On the same day, James Jeffords did indeed desert the Republican Party, throwing control of the U.S. Senate to the Democrats.[78]

June 6-8, 2001

President George W. Bush took his first plunge into the Middle East peace process by sending CIA Director George Tenet to Israel, in an effort to arrange a cease-fire between the Israelis and the Palestinians, so that the Mitchell Report could be implemented. On June 8 and 9, over twenty-eight inches of rain fell on the eastern portion of President Bush's home state of Texas. Altogether, from June 5-11, three feet of rain fell in the Houston Area. President Bush, who was vacationing at the time at his ranch in Crawford, Texas, declared 28 counties in Texas a federal disaster area.[79]

Many other such examples could be cited from history, or more recent current events. I have shared these few in an effort to stimulate thought, reflection, and prayer concerning the significance of God's words in Genesis 12:3, for America and for the nations in our generation. What I would submit to you is that Genesis 12:3 is indeed an eternally true statement of the Lord's intentions toward those who either bless or curse Israel. In my view, this Biblical exhortation and warning is as relevant today as it was in 2000 BC. If what I propose in this chapter is indeed true, then America would do well to rethink her current course in regard to U.S. policy on the Middle East.

As I wrote earlier in this book, I believe with all my heart that America has a special calling to bless Israel and the Jewish people. This calling is, I believe, a key aspect of God's redemptive purpose for our nation. Our adversary has done, is doing, and will continue to do, all he can to thwart the fulfillment of this element of America's redemptive purpose. An intense spiritual battle is being waged even now in the heavenly places above our beloved nation. In my view, this battle is on par with that described in chapter ten of the book of Daniel. To say that the stakes are high would be an understatement. Like Daniel, in this hour we too must fast and pray as never before for our country. Our future may very well hang in the balance.

History bears witness to the fact that no nation, people, or even individual has ever "cursed" God's chosen people and managed to escape God's wrath and judgment. And, they never will. May the United States of America never be among their number.

A PRAYER IN RESPONSE

*O Heavenly Father, we are sobered by the gravity of those words: "I will bless those who bless you, and whoever curses you, I will curse." And we are arrested by Your words through the prophet Joel, "I will gather **all nations** and bring them down to the Valley of Jehoshaphat. There I will enter into judgment against them concerning my inheritance, my people Israel, for they scattered my people among the nations and **divided up my land." (Joel 3:2) [Emphasis Added] Lord, because we love our country, we long to see America blessed by You. We ask you to keep the United States of America from committing dangerous errors in regard to Israel and the land. But more than our love of country, we love You. We long to bless You, Father, by blessing Your beloved and chosen people, Israel. For he who touches the Jewish people touches the apple of Your eye. (Zech. 2:8) Guide us, we pray. Guide our nation and her leaders. Speak to Your servants who serve in our government. Cause us to pray, and to listen, so that we will not miss Your will in this crucial area of dealing with Israel. In Jesus' Name, Amen.*

CHAPTER ELEVEN

The True Face of Islam

September 11, 2001 changed the United States — and the world — forever. Our nation will never be the same. The tragedy brought to the forefront of our national consciousness a threat that has been growing since the days of the Islamic revolution in Iran in the late 1970's. The horrors of militant Islam have arrived on our doorstep.

Islam currently controls or influences more than 50 countries in the world. Many of its most ardent adherents want to subjugate not just those 50 nations, but the remaining nations of the world as well. To be Sons of Issachar as we enter the 21st century, we as Christians must have an accurate understanding of Islam — its origins, ambitions, and strategies. To understand our time and to know what to do, we must fully grasp the nature of the spiritual battle looming before us.

Islam claims more than a billion adherents worldwide today. That is 20% of the world's population! Three hundred million Arab Muslims comprise about 25% of the world's total Muslim population.[80] Muslims comprise 35% of all currently unreached peoples, yet only 4% of the Church's missionary force is directed toward Muslim peoples. Instead of being evangelized, Muslims are evangelizing.

Saudi Arabia has given, and continues to give, millions of dollars to promote Islam in the United States and throughout the non-Islamic world. The state of New Mexico is the site of the first completely Islamic community in America, "Dar al Islam." The orthodox Sunni Muslims of that community intend to evangelize the United States.[81] Muslims have constructed more than 500 Islamic centers in America to serve as beachheads for "evangelism."

Already, Muslims outnumber Episcopalians in the U.S.[82] In Great Britain, more than 300 Anglican churches have been closed and then converted into mosques.[83] Many Muslims believe the United Kingdom will become the first Muslim country in Europe.[84] *Al-Islam*, an Islamic magazine in Germany, has reported that Muslims believe Europe, the cradle of the Reformation and the modern missions movement, will become Muslim within the next generation.[85]

Clearly, it is imperative that we as Christians understand the true face of Islam. As a starting point, let us first examine the "pillars of Islam." We will then briefly survey the origins and history of the religion.

THE "PILLARS" OF ISLAM

1. The creed, or *shahadah.* During prayers as well as many other times throughout the day, Muslims repeat the creed, "There is no god but Allah, and Mohammed is his prophet."

2. Prayer, or *salat.* Muslims are obliged to pray toward Mecca five times a day (at dawn, right after midday, two hours before sunset, right after sunset, and two hours after sunset).

3. Giving of alms, or *zakat.* Muslims are required to give the equivalent of 2.5% of their gross income to the poor.

4. Fasting, or *saum.* The most important Muslim fast takes place each year throughout the month of Ramadan. Muslims are supposed to fast from food, water, and sex from sunrise to sunset.

5. Pilgrimage, or *hadj.* Every adult Muslim should, if at all possible, journey to Mecca once during his lifetime if he is mentally and physically healthy and able to provide for his family during his absence.

6. Holy war, or *jihad.* Many Muslims also consider *jihad* to be a sixth pillar of Islam.[86]

JIHAD

Since September 11, 2001, much attention has been focused on this sixth pillar or *jihad*. Although it is often translated as "holy war," it literally means "struggle" or "exertion." *Jihad* always involves a call to battle against "evil," but it has several different expressions. *Jihad* of the heart parallels the Christian's battle with the flesh. *Jihad* of the mouth and pen defends and promotes Islam through both oral and written apologetics. *Jihad* of the hand promotes Islam through good deeds. *Jihad* of the sword refers to what is commonly known as "holy war." When *jihad* appears in the Qur'an standing alone, or with the phrase, "in the cause of Allah," it always refers to the call to actual physical warfare on behalf of Islam. This *jihad* is to continue as long as there are "infidels" who are not willing to submit to the authority of Islam. Mohammed himself endorsed and engaged in military *jihad*, and he ordered his followers to do likewise.[87]

Mohammed's concept of *jihad* changed over time as his circumstances warranted it. Islamic scholars have identified in the Qur'an four different stages in the development of the doctrine of *jihad:*

1. Peaceful Persuasion. This was the emphasis in the early days when Islam had few adherents. (Sura 16:125-126)

2. Self Defense. Fighting was permitted only to defend against aggression, or to reclaim stolen property. (Suras 22:39; 2:190-194)

3. Offense. Muslims were now allowed to initiate warfare except during the four sacred months of the Muslim calendar. (Sura 9:5)

4. No Limitations. All restrictions concerning war in the name of Allah were removed. (Sura 9:29)[88]

The Qur'an has 114 *suras,* or chapters, arranged from longest to shortest. If studied chronologically, a clear progression emerges confirming the development of hostility towards Jews and Christians. The earlier so-called Meccan suras (dating from 610-622 AD) are more tolerant of Christians and Jews, whereas the Medinan suras (from 622 AD onward), written later, are much more hostile in tone.[89] The fourth stage of understanding— or limitless *jihad* — is the one that has become normative for Islam.

The law of "abrogation" in Qur'anic hermeneutics (later revelation always supersedes that which precedes it if there is a conflict) supports this conclusion (2:106; 13:39; 16:101-102).[90] In addition to the Qur'an, the **Hadith** (written traditions of Mohammed) and the *"fatwa"* (a legal religious ruling) are authoritative for the Muslim. The Hadith confirms this understanding of *jihad* as well. One book of the Hadith quotes Mohammed as saying, "The last hour would not come until the Muslims fight against the Jews and the Muslims kill them; until the Jews hide themselves, and the stones and trees would speak up saying,...There is a Jew hiding behind me. Come and kill him" (Sahih Muslim, book 40, #6985).[91]

HISTORICAL OVERVIEW OF ISLAM

Having summarized the pillars of Islam, let us now take a brief tour through history, highlighting the origin and development of Islam, as well as its influence in world history.

570 — Mohammed is born into the Quraish tribe, which claims direct descent from Abraham through Ishmael. His father, Abdullah, dies near the time of his birth. His mother, Amina, dies when Mohammed is six years old. Mohammed is cared for briefly by his grandfather, the Chief of Mecca and keeper of the pagan shrine. He is then raised by his uncle, Abu Talib, the head of the prominent Hashim clan in Mecca. Mohammed becomes familiar with Judaism and Christianity while traveling with his uncle along Middle Eastern trade routes.[92]

610 — On the 17th of Ramadan, the angel Gabriel supposedly calls Mohammed to be a prophet of God. But Mohammed meets fierce resistance in polytheistic Mecca.

620 — Allah allegedly confirms Mohammed's status as a prophet, taking him by night to Jerusalem, where he talks with Jesus, Moses, and Abraham. He then ascends by ladder to the seventh heaven.

621 — Meccans still reject Islam. Mohammed flees to Medina.

622-630 — Unable to peacefully persuade his fellow Arabs to follow his new religion, Mohammed turns to violence. He battles his Arab enemies, finally taking Mecca in 630.[93]

Initially Mohammed shows tolerance for "people of the Book" — that is, Christians and Jews. He is convinced that both groups will soon recognize the purity of his revelations and convert to Islam. But as the Jews prove resistant to Mohammed's persuasion, he once again turns to violence. He forces out of Mecca two Jewish tribes who reject his prophetic claims. When a third tribe, the Qurayza, refuse to confirm his call, he annihilates them. Mohammed's military campaigns against fellow Arabs, the massacre of the Qurayza, and his raid into Syria late in his life, lay the foundation for future persecutions of Christians. The polemical nature of the Qur'an also provides religious justification for *jihad* against Christians, as the Muslim empire prepares to spread west toward Spain, north toward Constantinople, and east toward Asia.[94]

638 — The Caliph Umar defeats the Byzantines in Syria as well as the Persians. He takes Damascus and Jerusalem, as well as the Persian capital. Umar makes an agreement with the Christian and Jewish peoples living in the territories he conquers. The Pact of Umar establishes Jews and Christians as "*dhimmi*," or "protected persons." As such they must pay extra taxes to qualify for certain rights and guarantees of protection under Islamic law. However, in reality this "protection" actually translates into 2nd or 3rd class status, with rules guaranteed to gradually eradicate all religions but Islam. Under these laws, Christians are not allowed to:
1. Build new churches.
2. Repair old churches.
3. Manifest their religion openly or evangelize Muslims.
4. Wear Muslim garments.
5. Ride horses or bear arms.
6. Display crosses or Christian books along the roads or in the marketplaces of Muslims.
7. Marry Muslim women and raise children as Christians.

(Muslims, of course, are free to marry Christian women and raise the children as Muslims.)[95]

By 711 — Muslims control all of North Africa.

By 712 — Muslim invaders conquer much of Christian Spain.

717 — Muslim forces threaten "Christian" civilization in the East, invading southeast Europe, and besieging Constantinople. (If Constantinople had fallen, the Muslims might have overrun the entire continent, effectively Islamicizing Europe.)

732 — Charles Martel, the grandfather of Charlemagne, halts the Arab advance in the West at the Battle of Tours in France. (Once again, if the Muslims had not been defeated here, they likely would have conquered and Islamicized Europe.)

846 — Muslims attack the suburbs of Rome, the center of Christianity in the West. (This attack would be comparable to Christians raiding Mecca or Medina, which they have never done.)

1000 — Muslim ruler Hakim severely persecutes Jews and Christians in the Holy Land.

1009 — Hakim orders the destruction of the Church of the Holy Sepulcher in Jerusalem. The Christian population greatly declines due to the cruelty of Hakim's tyrannical rule.

Mid 11th Century — The Seljuk Turks conquer the Arabs but convert to Islam as they do so. The Turks turn out to be more tyrannical than the Muslim Arabs.

1071 — The Emperor Romanus Diogenes is defeated in the eastern Byzantine Empire. He loses all the territory that had been recovered in the 9th and 10th centuries. Succeeding Byzantine emperors appeal to the West for aid.[96]

1071 — The Seljuk Turks capture Jerusalem from the Shiite Fatimid dynasty of Egypt.

1091 — The Turks expel Christian priests from Jerusalem.

1095 — In the West, Pope Urban II launches the First Crusade in response to the dire straits of Eastern Christians.

1099 — The Crusaders conquer Jerusalem, massacring Jews and Muslims in the city.

1099-1291 — A "Christian" kingdom controls much of the Holy Land.

By 1187 — Famed Muslim ruler, Saladin, unites the Muslims of the Middle East and initiates a *jihad* against Christian rule in the Holy Land. In 1187, Saladin conquers Jerusalem.

1291 — All of the Holy Land is once again under Muslim control.[97]

14ᵗʰ Century — A new Muslim force arises: the Ottoman Turks. Once again a Muslim power launches an assault against Europe (through the Balkans).

1389 — Turks defeat Prince Lazar of Serbia.

1393 — Bulgaria falls to the Turks.

1448 — John Hunyadi of Hungary is defeated while trying to come to the aid of the Byzantines.

1453 — Constantinople, the capital of the Byzantine Empire in the East, falls.

Over the next two centuries, Western European strength grows to equal and then surpass that of the Islamic world.

1529 — Ottoman Turks besiege Vienna but are unable to take the city. (If Vienna had fallen, the Turks might very well have over-run Europe, effectively murdering the Reformation in its cradle. The Reformation had begun only twelve years earlier, in 1517.)

1683 — The Muslim Turks once again invade Western Europe, besieging Vienna for the second time. On the verge of collapse, Vienna is delivered by the Poles, led by Jan Sobieski.[98]

For 1,000 years — from the seventh to the seventeenth centuries — Christianity was under virtually continuous pressure from a militant Islamic advance. With the final defeat of the Turks in 1683, Islam retreated into seeming oblivion as a world force for 300 years. Then in 1979, the Ayatollah Khomeini led Islam out of her centuries-old identity crisis. The Islamic Revolution in Iran unleashed once again the threat of a revived, militant Muslim faith.[99] Khomeini began to mobilize energized Muslims on a quest to destroy the "Great Satan," the United States of America, and the "Little Satan," the state of Israel. The ultimate goal of this *jihad* is the subjection of the entire world to Islam and the dictates of Sharia law. As the Ayatollah Khomeini said, "The purest joy in Islam is to kill and be killed for Allah."[100]

Islam is a religion bent on world conquest and domination. Since its inception almost 1,400 years ago, Islam has advanced primarily by force — from the Arabian Peninsula to the far reaches of the globe. Its origins, practice, and history all testify to the true face of Islam.

A PRAYER IN RESPONSE:

Lord God Jehovah, we proclaim again that You are the only true God. We worship You, God the Father, God the Son, and God the Holy Spirit, the Triune god, creator of the heavens and the earth. You are the true God of Abraham, Isaac, and Jacob. Thank you for your Word, the Holy Scriptures, which You inspired and breathed into men, to write for all mankind to know. Thank you for Your sovereign hand, controlling the events of human history. Lord, we pray that You would make Yourself known in truth, to all people, and to all nations. Father, we ask You for mercy, that You would protect us from the danger of militant Islam, which seeks to conquer and subjugate the entire world. We ask You for mercy on the Jewish people, who are the object of especially focused hatred, fomented by Satan against the "apple of Your eye." And we ask you for mercy on the people and nations who are under the deception of the Muslim religion, and the oppressive power of an Islamic state. Open their eyes, that they may see Jesus. Empower and protect those who are serving as missionaries, Bible translators, and humanitarian aid workers in these lands. We pray that You would move in power to free the world from the grip and sway of this false religion. Help us to be Sons of Issachar who understand our times, and know what to do. Show us what You would have us do as the battle intensifies. Remind us always to pray, and to stay alert at our posts. Grant, in our day, that the knowledge of the glory of the Lord would indeed fill the earth as the water covers the sea (Habakkuk 2:14). Amen.

CHAPTER TWELVE

The Church and Militant Islam: Kingdoms in Conflict

A s the tentacles of Islamic fundamentalism continue to stretch over the face of the earth, what is at stake for the United States, Western Europe, and in fact, for civilization as we know it? What can we expect to see in the years ahead? What should be the response of the Church of the Lord Jesus Christ? What are the spiritual weapons at our disposal as we face this battle of epic proportions? This chapter will seek to address these pressing questions.

To answer them, however, we must first ask a more fundamental question: What is energizing the advance of Islam as it sweeps across the globe? Or, perhaps more simply stated, who is it that the Muslims actually worship?

Since September 11, 2001, we have heard countless times that the Muslims really worship the same God that Christians and Jews worship: the God of Abraham, Isaac, and Jacob; they just call him by a different name. Is this really true?

WHO IS ALLAH?
Is the god of Islam the God of the Bible? In a word, *no*. **The**

god of Islam is most definitely not the God we read about in the Old and New Testaments. Although it may not be "politically correct" to say so, I am going to say it anyway, because I believe it is "*spiritually* correct." From a Biblical perspective, the hard truth is that in reality, **the Muslims are worshipping a demon.** We must remember that according to I Corinthians 10:19-20, the "god" of any false religion is actually a demon: "Do I mean then that a sacrifice offered to an idol is anything, or that an idol is anything? No, but **the sacrifices of pagans are offered to demons, not to God,** and I do not want you to be participants with demons."

If Muslims are not worshipping the God of Abraham, Isaac, and Jacob, but rather a demon, who are they in fact serving? Muslims actually worship the **moon god** — or, rather I should say, the principality or the demon behind the moon god. When God called Abraham out of Ur of the Chaldees, the primary deity worshipped in that region was the moon god. The Syrians worshipped the moon god as well, but they called him "Sin" — not sin, as in wrongdoing, but rather a proper name for this god.[101] Interestingly enough, the symbol for this moon god was the crescent moon. Today, of course, the crescent moon is a well-known symbol of the Islamic faith. Its use as the primary identifying symbol of Islam on flags of Islamic nations and on the top of mosques and minarets harkens back to pagan Arabia, where Allah was worshiped as the moon god.[102]

Many pagan cultures of the ancient world worshipped a moon god. The Babylonian monarch, Nabu-na'id (Nabodnidus) placed the moon god at the top of the pantheon of Babylonian gods, renaming it "Bel." Nabu-na'id took this step in order to make the Babylonian religion more palatable to the Arabians and the Arameans living in his kingdom.[103] In ancient Arabia, the moon god was worshipped as "Al-Ilah." The contraction of these two words gives us the name "**Allah**."[104] Even at that time, Mecca was the religious center for the pagan religions of Arabia. Al-Ilah, the Arabian moon god, was considered to be the head god over 360 other deities. Al-Ilah was also known as the lord of the Kaaba, "the cube." The Kaaba housed a sacred black stone which the Quraish tribe believed was magical and offered them protection. It was most likely an asteroid that had fallen from the heavens at some point and was, therefore, believed to be sacred.[105] How significant that this is the same black stone venerated by Muslims today!

THE FOUNDATIONS OF ISLAM

As we explore its origins more thoroughly, we will see that Islam is nothing more than monotheistic paganism. When Mohammed founded Islam in the early seventh century, he did not in reality design a new faith as he claimed, but instead repackaged pagan beliefs that had been in existence for quite some time. In addition to the importance of Mecca and reverence for the Kaaba, other elements of what would become Islam also existed in ancient times. For example, pre-Islamic Arabians bowed and prayed toward Mecca at set times throughout the day. They also believed everyone should make a pilgrimage to Mecca at least once. Arabian pagans attached great significance to the giving of alms as well. They even fasted during the day and feasted at night one month out of the year. The pre-Islamic pagans also observed Friday as their "Sabbath." [106] All these future elements of Islam were already in place before Mohammed was ever born.[107]

Mohammed was born into the Quraish tribe in Arabia, a tribe devoted to the worship of Al-Ilah (or Allah), the moon god.[108] Mohammed repackaged Arabian heathenism as a monotheistic religion by taking the primary deity, the moon god, Al-Ilah, and declaring him to be the only god.[109] He also mixed together elements of Christianity and Judaism along with visions that he supposedly received from Allah in order to form this "new" religion. After an intense period of struggle and armed resistance, the Arabians finally succumbed to Mohammed's influence. The Arabians began to worship the moon god exclusively.

Since Mohammed considered Islam to be the only pure monotheistic faith, he expected the Jews to embrace it quickly. He considered Christianity and Judaism to be inferior religions. In his view, they had not achieved their purposes; therefore, God had birthed Islam as the complete and pure Faith. Mohammed considered Christians to be polytheists because from his point of view they worshipped three gods: God the Father, God the Son, and God the Holy Spirit. When his fellow monotheists, the Jews, rejected this new, more perfect monotheistic faith, Mohammed felt deeply betrayed. Over time he became increasingly filled with hatred towards the Jewish people. We will examine that development in greater depth later in this chapter.

DOES ISLAM MEAN "PEACE?"

Another often-repeated misconception about Islam is that the word itself means 'peace.' How many times since September 11ᵗʰ, 2001 have we heard that assertion, whether spoken by our President or by members of the news media. In point of fact, the word Islam does not mean peace! **A better translation would be 'submission.'**[110] **There is a big difference!** It could mean peace only in the sense of a peace that would come when the entire world is in submission to Islamic law. Linguistically, the word originally referred to the strength of a desert warrior willing to fight to the death for his tribe, even against impossible odds.[111] From that, we get the meaning 'submission,' and the seeds for the concept of *jihad* as well.

Islam — or, I should say, the demonic principality behind Islam — is not going to rest until Israel is driven into the sea, and "Christendom" is subject to Allah. Radical Islam's goal is to destroy not only the Jewish people, but America and Europe as well. The destruction of the 'Great Satan' (America) and the 'Little Satan' (Israel) is the stepping stone to replacing the Judeo-Christian world order with a fundamentalist Islamic world order. **That is the ultimate agenda of extremist Islam: the subjugation of the whole world to Islam.** The strategy calls for dealing with the Jews first, and then the "Christians." It has been reported that Muslims even have a song that they teach their young, summarizing this strategy: "Today Friday, tomorrow Saturday, then Sunday."[112] Friday is the holy day for the Muslims. Muslims are the 'Friday' people. They believe that they, as the 'Friday' people, will overcome the 'Saturday' people, the Jews, first and then the 'Sunday' people, the Christians. Then the whole world will become a 'Friday' people, in submission to Allah.

Again, the ultimate goal is subjugation of the world by force. According to Islam, there are only two types of people: Dar al-Islam, the domain of the faithful (adherents to Islam), and Dar Al-Harb, the domain of those with whom the faithful, the Muslims, are at war until Judgment Day (all non-Muslims).[113] To which category do we, as Christians, belong? To which category do the Jewish people belong? Clearly, those with whom the "faithful" are at war until Judgment Day. What a frightening prospect, especially given the fact that over the last 20 or 30 years, Muslims have moved *en masse* throughout the world. Did you know that there are more Muslims in Great Britain today than Methodists or Evangelical Christians?[114] Or that there are more Muslims in France than Protestants? Are you aware that some even claim that Muslims now outnumber Jews in the United States?[115]

I want to stress that I have nothing against the Muslim people themselves. Do not misunderstand me; please hear me clearly. I love the Muslim people. **I grieve for them because they have fallen prey to a grave deception.** They need Jesus as much as I do. We must always remember that our struggle is not against men: *"For our struggle is not against flesh and blood, but against the rulers, against the authorities, against the powers of this dark world and against the spiritual forces of evil in the heavenly realms."* (Ephesians 6:12) The Muslims are precious to God, yet they are demonically deceived and believe a lie. We as Christians are called to love them and pray for them. We must pray that the Lord would reveal to them the great deception behind Islam, and that they would see the truth, embracing their Savior, Jesus Christ.

What I write today, I write not out of any hatred, scorn, or contempt for the Muslims. On the contrary, I write all this out of compassion to see them not only saved for all eternity, but also liberated in *this* world by the power of Christ. Not one Islamic nation in the world has a truly democratic government. No Islamic country offers the same freedoms, or treasures the same values, as those societies that have been touched by the Judeo-Christian ethic. Islam is bent on one thing: the imposition of seventh-century Arabian culture on a modern 21st century world — whether that world wants it or not.[116]

THE QUR'AN COMMANDS VIOLENCE

Do not merely take my word for all this. Instead, I encourage you to read the Qur'an for yourself. **Go straight to the source** in order to find out what Islam is all about. Consider the following passages *from the Qur'an:*[117]

Sura 9:5 ('Sura' being the equivalent of 'chapter') says: "Fight and slay the pagans [the infidels — including Christians and Jews] wherever ye find them, and seize them, beleaguer them, and lie in wait for them in every stratagem of war."

If Islam is resisted, Sura 5:33 declares, "Their punishment is…execution, or crucifixion, or the cutting off of hands and feet from the opposite sides, or exile from the land."

Sura 8:59-61 adds: "Let not the unbelievers think they will ever get away…strike terror into the enemy of God and your enemy…rouse the faithful to arms! If they [the non-Muslims] incline to peace [accept Islam], make peace with them."

Sura 5:51 warns, "Believers [Muslims], take neither Jews nor Christians to be your friends: they are friends with one another. Whoever of you seeks their friendship shall become one of their number, and God does not guide [those Jewish and Christian] wrong-doers."

According to Suras 4:74 and 76, "Let those who would exchange the life of this world for the hereafter, fight for the cause of Allah; whether they die or conquer, we shall richly reward them….**The true believers** [Muslims] **fight for the cause of Allah, but the infidels** [Jews, Christians, and anyone else] **fight for their idols. Fight then against the priests of Satan.**" [Emphasis added]

Suras 9:14 and 29 exhort the faithful: "Fight them, Allah will punish them by your hands and bring them to disgrace….**Fight those who do not believe in Allah…until they pay the tax in acknowledgment of superiority and they are in a state of subjection.**" [Emphasis added]

And finally, Sura 5:49 declares, "If they reject your judgment, know that it is Allah's wish to scourge them for their sins."

These excerpts from the Qur'an should sober us all. Regardless of how moderate Muslim clerics spin it or the media mis-report it, this is what the Muslim holy book says. The force driving Islam today is not what the moderate Muslims believe; but rather what the extremist, fundamentalist Muslims believe.

THE GREAT CONFLICT OF OUR TIME

Undoubtedly the world faces a formidable a foe. We have only seen the opening volley of this war. September the 11th was only the beginning. Even if Al-Qaeda is liquidated and Osama bin Laden is caught, it will not be the end. In the previous generation, the epic battle was fought against atheistic Communism. **The battle of our generation will be fought against militant Islam.** What lies ahead is nothing less than the violent clash of two civilizations.

Although the struggle against Communism was ultimately a spiritual one, the battle was played out in the natural realm. We will not see much spiritual commentary written in the history books about the fall of Communism. In the same way, the battle looming before us, though it will be played out in the natural realm, will be pre-eminently spiritual in nature.

THE HISTORICAL AND SPIRITUAL SIGNIFICANCE OF ISLAMIC ADVANCES

To better understand the nature of the battle we face, how high the stakes are, as well as what our response needs to be, I would like to focus on two eras in history when Islam threatened to engulf the Western world. The Lord has been teaching me, over the last ten years, that we can learn a great deal from history; particularly if we investigate history led by the Holy Spirit. I believe the Lord can breathe on our study of particular eras in history, in order to teach us something for our current day. I'm convinced that is what the Lord is doing for us today.

Not long after Mohammed founded Islam in 610 AD, this new, yet old religion began its advance. By 638 the Muslims had captured Jerusalem, and soon thereafter they possessed Egypt, Syria, Mesopotamia, and Persia in a rapid expansion to the East. By 700 AD, Islam was sweeping across the west, virtually wiping out Christianity in North Africa.

The Muslims invaded Europe in 711, conquering most of Spain, and then moving into what is now Southern France. They had expanded to the east; they had expanded to the west. Then at the critical Battle of Tours in 732, Charles Martel, the Frankish king, turned back the Muslim onslaught. Martel was the grandfather of

Charlemagne, the first great emperor of what was called the Holy Roman Empire.[118]

To understand the full significance of the Battle of Tours, let us pause for a moment and take a look at what was happening in the Church and in Western Europe at that time. From a historical perspective, why would our adversary choose the late 7th and early 8th centuries to make this strategic attempt to wipe out Christianity?

By way of background, after Christianity became a protected religion, and then the official religion of the Roman Empire, Christianity actually spread very little beyond the borders of the Roman Empire. The prevailing attitude was that Christianity is for the civilized Romans, not for the barbarians. It was really only after the western Roman Empire fell in 476 AD that the Church saw a rebirth of apostolic impulse that lasted for several centuries.

In the 5th century, the renowned St. Patrick evangelized Ireland. By the late 6th century, Ireland was on the verge of a great age of Irish missionary activity, sending missionaries from Ireland to the European continent, which was largely pagan at that time.

At the time of Mohammed's birth and then the founding of Islam (late 6th and early 7th centuries), what was happening in Europe, as far as the advance of the gospel was concerned? Strategic inroads were being made into Spain, and portions of France, by Emilian and Samson. Columba brought the Gospel to northeast Scotland. Columbanus spread Christianity in France. In 596, Pope Gregory I sent a team of missionaries to convert the English to Christianity. In the early 7th century, Dark Age missionaries fanned out in many directions: Paulinus to Britain, Amandus to France, Fructuosus to Spain, Aidan to Britain, and Wilfred to Central Britain and Frisia (the Netherlands and modern Belgium).

What was happening in the 6th and 7th centuries? **The Gospel was on the move**, penetrating new frontiers in barbarian Europe.

Meanwhile, by the early 700's, Islam had swept across North Africa, and then pressed its advance first into Spain (711), and then into southern France. I would like to highlight one missionary in particular from this period. Boniface is one of the best-known of the missionaries of the Dark Ages. He received a papal commission to preach the Gospel east of the Rhine, and he was formally under the protection of Charles Martel, who was also known as "The Hammer."

Boniface moved eastward to carry the Gospel into what we now know as Germany during the period 723 to 738. Christian history now knows Boniface as the "Apostle to Germany." His strategic vision and tireless efforts inspired missionary work not only in the 8th century, but through the 9th, 10th, and 11th centuries as well! What a man of God!

Where was Boniface from 723 to 738? Pioneering the Gospel advance in Germany. What was the enemy's counter-move? Here come the militant Muslims. They invaded France, attacking the Frankish king, Charles Martel, under whose protection Boniface was spreading the Gospel to the east. Do you understand the significance of this scenario? **The enemy was using an Islamic assault in an effort to thwart the powerful missionary advances of the Gospel.**

Imagine if Charles Martel had lost? What if Islam had successfully overrun France? Western and Northern Europe would not now be Christian. *Islam, not Christianity, would have been the primary worldview that would have shaped western and northern Europe for more than 1,000 years.* Europe would have been Islamicized, not Christianized. Pause for a moment and reflect on that last statement. Europe would have been Islamicized, not Christianized. **It was a crucial moment in the history of mankind,** and in the history of the spiritual battle in the heavenly places.

After Charles Martel's victory and the halt of militant Islam, Charlemagne became the first Emperor of the Holy Roman Empire in 768. He expanded his kingdom eastward, encouraging missionary endeavors among the unreached of Germany, as well as the strengthening of the faith of the Franks. Were some of the missionary tactics, unfortunately, not what we would sanction today? Yes. Were there forced conversions at times? Yes. Was it a mixed record? Yes. But, were there also men like Boniface and other Dark Age missionaries who carried the true Gospel forward into Europe? Yes! What do you think would have happened to Boniface if the Muslims had conquered France and Germany? Christianity in Europe would have been strangled in its cradle.

After Boniface, Anskar, the Apostle to the North, pioneered missionary work in Denmark and Sweden in the 9th century.[119] The brothers Methodius and Cyril evangelized Moravia and Bulgaria.[120] In the 10th and 11th centuries, Northern Europe and Scandinavia were penetrated by the Gospel, and from the 12th to the 14th centuries, Eastern Europe and the Baltics were reached as well.

In retrospect, through the eyes of history, we see an era of great missionary activity, and a counterattack of our adversary aimed at halting the missionary advance of the Gospel.

Satan saw that a great harvest had begun, and that an even greater harvest lay ahead. So he, and all his demonic hordes, animated militant Islam in an attack against Europe. Praise the Lord, our God turned back the tide in 732. Charles Martel won the victory in the natural realm, and that is what is recorded in the history books. But what we, as believers and as Sons of Issachar, need to see is that it was a victory first and foremost in the heavenly places. A victory that made possible, in the natural realm, the advance of Christianity into areas previously unreached by the Gospel.

Let us fast-forward now to the 15th and 16th centuries. Once more, Islam was on the move threatening western Christianity, this time by an invasion from the east. In 1453, Constantinople, the capital of the Byzantine Empire (the Eastern Roman Empire), fell to the Ottoman Turks. Again the Muslims advanced westward, besieging Vienna in 1529. Just as in 732, the Muslim invaders were halted, and the threat to Europe from militant Islam greatly subsided.

Again, we must ask, **"What is the significance of the *timing?*** Why was militant Islam on the march again? What had been happening in Europe? What was God doing?"

What had happened in 1517? Martin Luther had nailed his Ninety-Five Theses to the door of the Wittenburg Church, sparking the Reformation and the rediscovery of long-lost Biblical truths: *sola Scriptura* (Holy Scripture is our sole authority), *sola fide* (salvation by faith alone), and *sola gracia* (salvation by grace alone)! These mottoes of the Protestant Reformation summarized a fresh, more Biblically accurate understanding of the Scriptures and the new birth. To receive salvation, a man must personally repent and receive by faith Jesus Christ as his Savior and Lord. Such a rediscovery of Biblical truth was both essential and radical for the

16th century Church. In 1529, the Reformation was only twelve years old. **What was the devil's objective? Once again to use militant Islam to strike at the heart of Europe, destroying this infant Reformation in its cradle.**

Imagine what would have happened if the advance of the Ottoman Turks had succeeded? Islam would have swept Europe on its second attempt, supplanting Christianity as the dominant religion in the west. Once again, however, the Lord intervened. He stemmed the tide, protecting the advance of the Reformation — a Reformation that would pave the way for the modern missions movement. **It is only as a result of the Reformation's influence that the Puritan awakening of the 17th century so greatly impacted England, and our own country as well.** I wrote in earlier chapters about the spiritual heritage of our nation and the legacy of our spiritual grandfathers, the Puritans. In all likelihood, there would haven been no Puritan Awakening if the Reformation had not succeeded. *Imagine how different the history of the world might have been if the tide of Islam had not been turned back at the gates of Vienna in 1529.* The ramifications are staggering indeed.

We must have discernment to see the spiritual battle that has raged on the pages of history and now rages before our very eyes. We must ask God to help us see not only what is happening in the natural realm, but especially what is happening in the spiritual realm.

The Puritan awakening of the 17th century was followed by the Moravian revival of the 18th century. A 24-hour-a-day prayer watch, begun under the leadership of Nicholas Ludwig von Zinzendorf, lasted for 100 years and spawned great missionary endeavors that changed the world. Moravian missionaries were instrumental in the conversions of both John Wesley and George Whitefield, men greatly used of God in the great 18th century awakenings in England and America.[121] The Great Century of Missions followed in the 19th century, and in the 20th century we have seen enormous strides made toward the fulfillment of the Great Commission, particularly among previously unreached people groups. These centuries of advance for the Gospel were made possible by the success of the Reformation.

THE MODERN RESURGENCE OF ISLAM

Twice, Islam had seemed to be on the verge of overtaking the world; twice it was turned back, failing to fulfill its destiny as outlined by the Qur'an. As a result of this second failure, Islam, as a militant force, retreated into a 400-year destiny crisis. Then in the 1970s — enter Ayatollah Khomeini, the Iranian spiritual leader. Khomeini recast a vision for the destiny of the Muslim people. He explained their failures as stemming from a lukewarm attitude towards the Jews. His basic message was, "We will succeed — Allah will grant us success — if we destroy Israel. We've failed because we haven't done so. **When we destroy Israel, the subjugation of the entire world will follow."**

So yet once more in our own generation, the enemy is breathing his demonic power into one of his favorite vessels. Interestingly enough, Ayatollah Khomeini's name bears a striking resemblance to that of the ancient prime minister of Persia, "Haman." If you will remember the story of Esther, Haman was the channel through whom the enemy hatched a diabolical plot to wipe out all the Jews in the Persian Empire. Is that a coincidence? No. The "Prince of Persia" — this demonic prince, of whom we know very little, but who is mentioned in the book of Daniel — is alive and well. He still seeks to thwart the purposes of God in our day, just as he did in Daniel's day.

I believe the same spirit that animated or demonized Haman also demonized the Ayatollah Khomeini. And he demonizes others today. Why? **Because the enemy sees something that perhaps many Christians don't have eyes to see!** God forgive us. The devil sees the success that the Gospel has experienced over this last generation. He sees the possibilities of even greater success for the advance of the kingdom of Christ in the days ahead. As a result, he is mobilizing the hordes of hell against it!

How does our enthusiasm, our fervor as believers in the Gospel, compare to that of these Muslim fundamentalists, who would die — and who are dying readily — for a lie? Will we die for the truth? They give their all for a lie, in an effort to subjugate the world. Will we give our all to humbly take the truth to that same world? There is always a new frontier, Beloved. There was in the

Dark Ages. There was at the time of the Reformation. And there is a new frontier today, perhaps the final frontier: touching the remaining unreached peoples of the world with the Gospel of Jesus Christ.

In an earlier chapter I discussed Romans 11, the significance of Israel's physical and spiritual restoration, and the connection to the advance of the Gospel. You will remember we highlighted the importance of the years 1948 (year of the re-establishment of the modern state of Israel) and 1967 (year of the Jewish liberation of Jerusalem). You may remember as well some statistics I cited concerning the expansion of Christianity. More Jews have embraced Jesus as the Messiah since 1967 than from the 4th century to 1967.[122] More Jews have been saved in a generation than were saved in 1,600 years. Could such a sudden and radical change be a coincidence? We have also seen more Muslims saved since 1980 than in the past 1,000 years. And, we have seen breakthroughs among many unreached people groups in what is known as the "10/40 Window." Again, could such a sudden harvest be a coincidence?

Even now the Body of Christ is mobilizing more people than ever before to pray for, and to reach, these unreached peoples. God is moving. He has been moving. But more is on the way. I believe it with all my heart! So, what is the enemy doing? What is his strategy for yet a third time? He sees a missionary advance, even greater than that of the Dark Ages or in the aftermath of the Reformation. As a result, he is coming against the Church, with all the furor that he can unleash. Once again his chosen vessel is militant Islam. Beloved, the battle before us is epic in proportion. **To say that the stakes are high would be a gross understatement.** I believe that our generation — our generation! — is like those of Boniface and Luther. We cannot remain apathetic, indifferent, or complacent. To be spiritually comatose could prove to be fatal. We must not take this threat lightly.

OUR RESPONSE – AS A "HEZEKIAH GENERATION"

You may say, "Very well, what do we do? What must we do? What are our weapons? Do we deploy a missile shield?" Yes, I think we probably should. But in reality, most likely "the best defense is a good offense." So then, "Do we take the battle abroad, and root out terrorism where we can?" Certainly. "Do we stockpile vaccines against biological weapons?" Of course. "Do we step up security at home?" Most definitely. We should do all these things, looking at the situation from the natural perspective.

But I fear that if that is all we do, a day may come when all our best efforts will not be enough. So, what do we do? Where do we turn for God's word of wisdom for this hour?

Once again, I believe God desires to speak to us through the life of Hezekiah. **His generation, I believe, is <u>analogous</u> to our own, as we face a third onslaught of Islam.** Let's look at his reign again.

The great revival of Hezekiah's day took place against the backdrop of an imminent Assyrian threat. The Assyrian kingdom had destroyed the northern kingdom of Israel in 722 BC, in the sixth year of Hezekiah's reign. (II Kings18:10) Hezekiah and all the people of Judah had a front-row seat to Israel's demise. I am convinced that the Lord used the destruction of the northern kingdom, and the threat of an Assyrian assault against the southern kingdom, to scare the people of Judah to death! **A holy fear prepared their hearts for revival,** and **caused them to be more open to look at their sin.**

Interestingly enough, the Assyrian king had a name that is very significant for our purposes. Sennacherib means "Sin [the moon god] has substituted for my brother."[123] Sennacherib killed his brother and usurped the Assyrian throne. Likewise, that is what is happening in our day. The radical Muslims seek to kill their ethnic brothers, the Jews, and usurp their place, in order to rule the world. I believe God is showing us through the Scriptures a Biblical, historical parallel of the demonic attacks that we face today.

This generation is also instructive for us in terms of a Biblical response to the threat before us. "Sin" (the moon god) was animated by a demon then, and Allah (the moon god) is animated by a demon today. The goal is the same. One way or another, "Sennacherib" is coming. The tide of Islam will crest and crash against the shores of the western world.

How do we respond? The answer is so simple! **We do what Hezekiah did. We fear the Lord! We seek His favor**.

How? First of all, we humble ourselves before the Lord, so that we will not have to be humiliated.

Secondly, we repent of our sin. If nothing else, we Christians need to **repent of an apathy** that is choking us to death. Apathy has the power to choke "Christendom" to death. We ought to stand convicted before the examples of these Muslim warriors, who will give everything for a lie — when we will give so little for the truth. How much time do we spend praying for the advance of the Gospel? How much of our resources do we give for the advance of the Gospel? How willing are we to be embarrassed to broach the Gospel? How willing are we to become foreign missionaries ourselves? God forgive us! God forgive us! We need to repent. Not only of such selfishness, but of any of the other sins, our "pet sins," that the Lord would convict us of individually. Like Hezekiah, we too must get the "rubbish out of our temples." We must cleanse our lives and our churches. Every offense and abomination to the Lord must go. Our lives and the life of our nation depend on it!

Thirdly, we need to consecrate ourselves to the Lord, as holy, living sacrifices. God is warning us that judgment begins with the house of God (I Peter 4:17). We must remain in the world, yet get rid of the world in us. God is calling us to be holy, as He is holy (I Peter 1:15-16).

Fourthly, we need to return to our Biblical and historical roots. We need to "ask for the ancient paths." We can learn valuable lessons from the generations of Hezekiah, and our Puritan forebears. This counsel can literally be used of the Lord to deliver us in the face of many dangers. What God has shown us as Sons of Issachar, we must share with others. We need to be repentant heralds, faith-filled harbingers of hope.

Lastly, as a repentant people, acknowledging our abject dependence on God, we need to cry out for mercy and deliverance, as did Hezekiah (II Kings 19:15-19; Isaiah 37:16-20). His cry ought to be our cry — but it will only be powerful if it is the prayer of a truly repentant people:

> O LORD, God of Israel, enthroned between the cherubim, you alone are God over all the kingdoms of the earth. You have made heaven and earth. Give ear, O

LORD, and hear; open your eyes, O LORD, and see; listen to the words Sennacherib has sent to insult the living God. It is true, O LORD, that the Assyrian kings have laid waste these nations and their lands. They have thrown their gods into the fire and destroyed them, for they were not gods but only wood and stone, fashioned by men's hands. Now, O LORD our God, deliver us from his hand, so that all kingdoms on earth may know that you alone, O LORD, are God.

The kingdoms of the earth knew, in 732. The kingdoms of the earth knew in 1529. The kingdoms of the earth knew in 701 BC, because Hezekiah feared the Lord and sought His favor. Hezekiah repented. Hezekiah led his people to repent; and a repentant people prayed. How did the Lord respond? He sent an angel, who slew 185,000 members of the Assyrian army, a force against which Judah stood no chance in the natural. Sennacherib withdrew in disgrace to Assyria. Later, while worshipping a false god in a pagan temple, he was killed by two of his own sons. What an ignominious end for one who threatened the nations and kingdoms of the ancient near East!

Our hope is this: if we respond to the Lord, I believe the He will deliver us as He did Judah. He will pour out His mercy, His grace, and His saving power. "Sennacherib" is no match for the living God!

According to Jeremiah, the prophet Micah warned Hezekiah and his generation that judgment was coming. He prophesied doom to the house of Judah. But, Jeremiah also records Hezekiah's response to this prophetic word of warning from the Lord. Hezekiah feared the Lord, and sought His favor. Let me say that again: **Hezekiah feared the Lord, and sought His favor**. As a result, "**The LORD relented** concerning the doom which he had pronounced against them" (Jeremiah 26:19). What merciful words! But not only that — what grace! Not only did Hezekiah's generation not know judgment, but instead, it experienced what was arguably the greatest revival in the history of the kingdoms of Israel and Judah! According to Scripture, there was never a king like Hezekiah, before him or after him. The temple was cleansed, and idols were smashed throughout the kingdom. His response to the

Lord bore great fruit: revival instead of judgment, and deliverance instead of destruction. The Lord then granted Hezekiah great wealth as well as rest on every side from his enemies.

May God give us such understanding of the times and seasons. May He give us wisdom to receive His strategy for deliverance and for prayer. May He give us the grace to repent, and to pray as we have never prayed, seeking the Lord as a repentant people, for deliverance in the spiritual battle of our age. May we pray as well for the spiritual deliverance of the peoples of the earth who do not yet know Jesus, but will benefit from the increase of this next advance for the Gospel. We have a destiny, Beloved! We have a destiny in the Lord if we will claim it! If we will embrace it by faith, in the fear of the Lord. And if we will move in obedience, prayer, and faithfulness, as He leads us. The God of King Hezekiah is my God, and He is your God, too. Our God is the same yesterday, today, and forever. Blessed be His mighty and glorious Name!

A PRAYER IN RESPONSE

Almighty Father in heaven, thank You for Your Word, in which is all truth, in which is all understanding, in which is every Biblical strategy needed for prayer. Thank You that You offer us hope, even as You call us to faith and challenge us — even command us — to repent. Thank You that though You are holy and must judge, You are also merciful and gracious. Thank You that as You warned Hezekiah, and his generation, so You warn us. Father, I pray more than anything else that we would be like Hezekiah — that we would fear You and seek Your favor. Would You hear our cry as Your repentant people, acknowledging our abject dependence on You. Would You deliver us in the great battle that looms ahead, not only for Your Name's sake, but that a great Gospel advance would not be clipped. May we see an even greater advance, particularly among a humbled Muslim people, who would be ready to receive the truth, having seen the lie of Islam exposed. May Your kingdom advance in the hearts and minds of all unreached peoples of the world. O Father, don't let us sleep! Don't let us slumber any more! It's time to awaken, and to pray with conviction for the souls of this nation, and for the souls of all nations! God, grant us Your heart; grant us

Your fervor. May Your passion beat in our breast as it did in Hezekiah's. O, that we would fear You and seek You as he did. O, that we would know Your mercy and Your grace, through deliverance — a deliverance of Biblical proportions! Sovereign Lord, demonstrate Your power in this hour that once again the kingdoms of the earth would know that You alone are God! In the name of Jesus, the King of Kings and Lord of Lords, Amen.

CHAPTER THIRTEEN

For Such a Time as This

"*Blessed condescension.*" That was the phrase that gripped my heart recently during a time of worship and prayer. It is a phrase that describes our Lord's continual initiation in His relationship with us. As I ponder these words, I am struck by two thoughts. First of all, I am amazed that the Lord would condescend to save me — that He would stoop as low as He did for you and me, when we do not deserve it. Secondly, I am awestruck by the fact that not only did He stoop to grant us so sweet a salvation, but He also continues to stoop in order to speak to us. Over the last few years as I have sought the Lord, He has, I believe, condescended to speak to my heart in a blessed way. That is not something that I take lightly. I believe that we can indeed hear from the Lord when we earnestly seek Him, believing that He speaks and that He delights to condescend. Not just to save us, but to commune with us.

AN ORDINARY MAN…AN EXTRAORDINARY GOD

James tells us that the prophet Elijah was a man like us. When he prayed, the Lord shut the heavens for three years. When he prayed again, the Lord opened the heavens once more. (James 5:17-18) To us, Elijah was a great man of God, a hero of the faith. We find it difficult to grasp the truth that he was indeed "a man just like us." The truth is that Elijah was indeed ordinary; His God, however, was, and is, extraordinary. I have undertaken to write this book as one ordinary man whose heart has been touched by God. One of the beautiful aspects of the character of our God is that He delights to use ordinary vessels. We do not have to be an "Elijah" to hear from God. He stoops to speak to the "least" of us, for His extraordinary nature is all the more brilliant in the lives of ordinary men and women.

Whom did Jesus choose to use in the miracle of the feeding of the 5,000, but a young boy who was willing to give the Lord his lunch. It was not much — just five loaves and two fish, but O, what our Lord can do with just five loaves and two fish. As I reflected on this miracle, the Lord reminded me of three simple characteristics of that young boy. Three things that I desire to characterize my life, and that I hope will characterize your lives, especially after having read the testimony that is this book.

First of all, the young boy **drew near** to see Jesus. He chose to come to where Jesus was; he chose to **enter into His presence**. That is a choice we all can make. It is from that choice that every-thing else flows. Secondly, he came **expecting** that Jesus would speak to him. He knew that he would hear from Jesus. We, too, can learn to approach Jesus with expectant, listening hearts, if we choose to. Lastly, this young boy **responded** to Jesus, giving Him his lunch. He knew it was not much, of course, but he gave it anyway, offering all he had.

What did our Lord Jesus Christ do with the lunch of one boy? He blessed it, He broke it, and then He fed multitudes with it. Five thousand men, not including women and children, ate and were satisfied. Not only that, but after this massive luncheon by the Galilee, the disciples collected 12 basketfuls of leftovers. Now, I would call that a Class-A miracle! We need such a miracle today in the Church and in our nation. I don't know about you, but I want to be like that boy. I long for the Lord to take my life, break it, bless it, and feed multitudes with it. I yearn for the Lord to take my life like a thread, and weave it together with the lives that have come before, and those that will come after, into an amazing tapestry that depicts the history of the advance of the kingdom of God.

In this last chapter, I hope to both encourage and exhort you to offer the Lord your "lunch." To allow Him to weave the thread of your life into the Lord's kingdom tapestry of this generation. What miracle might the Lord perform in our day if enough of us were willing to part with a few loaves and some fish? God has sown much into the spiritual fabric of this nation, and I do not believe He is finished with us yet. I believe with all my heart that the United States of America still has a purpose in the heart of God that she has not yet fulfilled.

A VISION FOR AMERICA'S DESTINY

Let me share with you the words of some others who have felt the same way. Ronald Reagan, the fortieth president of the United States, once said of America, "I have always believed that this anointed land was set apart in an uncommon way, that a divine plan placed this continent here between the oceans to be found by people from every corner of the earth who had a special love of faith and freedom." [124] Reagan's favorite description of America was that of a "shining city upon a hill." Is it a coincidence that Ronald Reagan would speak that way of the United States? Or was he, in some sense, speaking prophetically — and by that I mean, uttering a message of divine significance — whether he knew it or not? Is it a coincidence when secular leaders notice the threads of God's purposes running through our history? I believe that such comments reveal a scarlet thread of God's redemptive purpose for our country that our Lord — the Master Weaver — has woven and continues to weave into the tapestry of our history.

President Calvin Coolidge echoed similar sentiments to those of Ronald Reagan, in 1923. "It has often been said that God sifted the nations, that He might send choice grain into the wilderness [of America]. Who can fail to see in it the hand of destiny? Who can doubt that it [the United States] has been guided by the hand of God?" [125]

That guidance has been clear throughout our history, perhaps never more so than at the time of the Revolutionary War. Apart from divine intervention, the colonists would most certainly have lost the war. How could a ragtag group of mostly volunteers have withstood the might of the British Army? Listen to the answer as expressed by Benjamin Franklin at the Constitutional Convention in 1787. Reminding those gathered there of God's supernatural intervention in the Revolutionary War, Franklin declared:

> In the beginning of the contest with Britain, when we were sensible of danger, we had daily prayer in this room for the Divine protection. Our prayers, Sir, were heard, and they were graciously answered. All of us who were engaged in the struggle must have observed frequent instances of a superintending Providence in our favor. To that kind Providence we owe this happy opportunity of consulting in peace on the means of establishing our future national felicity."[126]

President Harry Truman once said, "I do not think anyone can study the history of this nation of ours without becoming convinced that Divine Providence has played a part in it. I have a feeling that God has created us and brought us to our present position of power and strength for some great purpose."[127] What is this great purpose? In this book, I have presented four aspects of that great purpose:

- To be a *"redeemer nation,"* a lighthouse to the nations for the Gospel.
- To be a *"shining city on a hill,"* a New Covenant community, living out the New Covenant way — loving God and loving one another.
- To be a *"promised land,"* a haven and a refuge for the oppressed and downtrodden.
- And, lastly, to be a *blessing to Israel* and the Jewish people.

IS AMERICA FULFILLING HER DESTINY?

If God has indeed brought us to a position of strength for a great purpose, how are we doing, particularly as we look back over the last generation? The American author John Steinbeck once said, "If I wanted to destroy a nation, I would give it too much; and I would have it on its knees, miserable, greedy, and sick."[128] It could be said that no nation has been as blessed as the United States of America. But is it possible that we have become <u>too</u> blessed, and that we now take our blessings for granted? That we now worship the gifts instead of the Giver? That we are now more committed in our country to building the house of the American Dream, rather than restoring the house of God? Are we more committed to building our own personal kingdoms, or are we committed, as citizens of the kingdom heaven first, and citizens of America second — to building God's kingdom?

Moses had these words of warning for the children of Israel in Deuteronomy 8:11-14, 17-19:

> Beware that you do not forget the LORD your God by not keeping His commandments, His judgments, and His statutes which I command you today, lest — when you have eaten and are full, and have built beautiful houses and dwell in them; and when your herds and your flocks multiply, and your silver and your gold are multiplied, and all that you have is multiplied; when your heart is lifted up, and you forget the LORD your God...[and] then you say in your heart, 'My power and the might of my hand have gained me this wealth.' And you shall remember the LORD your God, for it is he who gives you power to get wealth, that he may establish His covenant which he swore to your fathers, as it is to this day. Then it shall be, if you by any means forget the LORD your God, and follow other gods, and serve them and worship them, I testify against you this day that you shall surely perish. (NKJV)

These words were addressed to the ancient nation of Israel; nevertheless, the principles, I believe, could apply to our nation, or to any nation. We dare not assume in a complacent, pseudo-Christian arrogance that America is somehow exempt from such a fate. We would do well to heed the message of the prophet Jeremiah:

> If at any time I announce that a nation or kingdom is to be uprooted, torn down or destroyed [*notice this declaration*

is not limited to Israel], and if that nation repents of its evil, then I will relent and not inflict on it the disaster I had planned. And if at another time I announce that a nation is to be built up or planted, and if it does evil in my sight and does not obey me, then I will reconsider the good I had intended to do for it. (Jeremiah 18:7-10)

As the American Civil War raged on, President Abraham Lincoln described our national tendency toward such forgetfulness as described above:

We have been the recipients of the choicest bounties of heaven. We have been preserved these many years in peace and prosperity; we have grown in numbers, wealth, and power as no other nation has ever grown. But we have forgotten God. We have forgotten the gracious hand which preserved us in peace and multiplied and enriched and strengthened us, and we have vainly imagined, in the deceitfulness of our hearts, that all these blessings were produced by some superior wisdom and virtue of our own. Intoxicated with unbroken success, we have become too self-sufficient to feel the necessity of [God's] redeeming and preserving grace, too proud to pray to the God that made us! [Proclamation, March 30, 1863][129]

President Lincoln also warned, "If danger ever reaches us, it must spring up from amongst us. It cannot come from abroad. If destruction be our lot, we must ourselves be its author and finisher."[130] I believe Abraham Lincoln was correct. It is our grievous national sins that have separated us from God and could ultimately result in our destruction. As the prophet Isaiah said, "Surely the arm of the LORD is not too short to save, nor his ear too dull to hear. But your iniquities have separated you from your God; your sins have hidden his face from you, so that he will not hear." (Isaiah 59:1-2).

Inscribed on the walls of the Jefferson Memorial are these solemn words of Thomas Jefferson: "God who gave us life gave us liberty. Can the liberties of the nation be secure when we have removed a conviction that these liberties are the gift of God? Indeed I tremble for my country when I reflect that God is just, that His justice cannot sleep forever!"

During the Korean War, in December 1951, General Douglas MacArthur exhorted his fellow Americans:

> In this day of gathering storm, as the moral deterioration…spreads its infection…**it is essential that every spiritual force be mobilized to defend and preserve the religious base on which this nation was founded.** For it is that base that has been the motivating impulse to our moral and national growth. History fails to record a single precedent in which nations subject to moral decay have not passed into political and economic decline. **There has been either a spiritual re-awakening to overcome the moral lapse, or a progressive deterioration leading to ultimate national disaster.** [131] (Emphasis added)

SEPTEMBER 11, 2001 — A WAKE-UP CALL

The dustbin of history is filled with the ashes of once-great civilizations! September the 11th was a clear warning to us, to the Church, and to the country, not to rely on our perceived greatness. In one day, the symbols of our economic strength and our military prowess were either damaged or destroyed, and our intelligence services were without a clue. As I sat watching the television on the afternoon of September 11th, the Lord brought to my mind Jeremiah 9:23-24:

> This is what the LORD says: 'Let not the wise man boast of his wisdom or the strong man boast of his strength or the rich man boast of his riches, but let him who boasts boast about this: that he understands and knows me, that I am the LORD, who exercises kindness, justice and righteousness on earth, for in these I delight,' declares the Lord.

On that horrific day, our knowledge failed us. We saw what could one day happen to our economy, and even to our military capacities. Knowledge can and will fail us. Our economy can and perhaps will fail us. Even our military strength could possibly fail us at some point. None of these is capable, in an ultimate sense, of protecting us or preserving us.

Yet, in spite of everything that has happened, I believe the Lord has heard the prayers of a remnant, and has opened a doorway of mercy. A doorway into the throne room of God. The King is sitting on His throne, extending His scepter and beckoning us to enter that doorway. The question for us, as American Christians, is: **What will we do at this moment in history?**

"FOR SUCH A TIME AS THIS"

I hope that we will arise and respond as did Mordechai and Esther in the 5ᵗʰ century BC. Like us, Mordechai and Esther lived in a prosperous generation, during which an unexpected peril arose. In Esther and Mordechai's day, the Jewish people had already been restored to the land. God was renewing and reviving the remnant that had returned to the land of Judah. Throughout the Persian kingdom, however, lived many more Jewish people who had decided not to return to the land. They had become prosperous and chose not to return. Mordechai and Esther were among this number. Esther, the orphaned Jewess, rose to become the queen of the Persian Empire, the greatest empire on the earth at that time. Her cousin, Mordechai, served in the king's court. They were prosperous. They were successful. What could possibly go wrong?

Haman, the Persian prime minister, devised a diabolical plot to destroy the Jewish people throughout the empire. Haman's plot parallels the enemy's agenda in our day: to destroy the Jewish people, and to destroy the Judeo-Christian order as we know it, replacing it with a fundamentalist Islamic order. The Ayatollah Khomeini, who recast the destiny of the Muslim people in the 1970s, even has a name that is very similar to "Haman." We can learn much from the book of Esther, as we look at our own generation — a generation that has also known great prosperity since the last "-ism" — Communism — fell. But, a new "-ism" is rising, and it is Islamic Fundamentalism. Here comes Haman once again.

Having learned of Haman's plot, Mordechai comes to Esther,

and implores her to go seek the favor and intervention of the king. Initially, Esther is reluctant and afraid; she does not want to compromise her position, or perhaps even lose her life. (Is there a parallel here to our apathy and selfishness today?) Yet Mordechai wisely reminds her of what is clearly now God's vision for her life:

> "Do not think in your heart that you will escape in the king's palace any more than all the other Jews. For if you remain completely silent at this time, relief and deliverance will arise for the Jews from another place, but you and your father's house will perish. Yet who knows whether you have come to the kingdom for such a time as this?" (Esther 4:13 NKJV).

Beloved, we too have come to this generation in our nation's history, and in the history of the world, **for such a time as this.** We are all alive at this hour by God's providence.

How does Esther respond? "Go, gather all the Jews who are present in Shushan and fast for me; neither eat nor drink for three days, night or day. My maids and I will fast likewise. And so I will go to the king, which is against the law; and if I perish, I perish." (Esther 4:16) With her people facing perhaps the most dangerous crisis in their history, Esther turns to the Lord in fasting and prayer. How instructive for the Body of Christ in this hour!

We are all familiar with the rest of the story. Esther fulfills her divine calling. Haman is hanged on the very gallows he had constructed for Mordechai. King Xerxes issues a new decree, providing for the defense of the Jewish people. Mordechai even becomes the new Prime Minister. The account of Esther is indeed a beautiful story of triumph for the Jewish people.

SYMBOLISM IN THE BOOK OF ESTHER

As in the book of Ruth, so also in the book of Esther we see symbolism that is very rich in meaning for our generation. For example, I believe Esther is a picture of the Body of Christ. She is married to Xerxes, the Persian king. So, too, we as believers are married to the "king" — the King of kings, in fact! As Xerxes beckoned to Esther to enter his presence, so the Lord Jesus Christ is calling us — the Church — into His presence! Our king, Jesus Christ, ever lives to intercede for us (Hebrews 7:25). As the bride of Christ, we are called to join in that intercession.

Mordechai symbolizes the Holy Spirit. As Mordechai approached Esther, so the Holy Spirit comes to us, particularly at this time of crisis in our nation, saying, "Don't just sleep in the palace, luxuriating in your prosperity. Don't think that you — Church, in America — will escape! You have been raised up, just like Esther, for such a time as this. You, too, are called to go to your King, in a spirit of fasting and prayer, that He would issue a decree for your deliverance."

God uses human vessels to fulfill God-sized purposes. The Holy Spirit is calling. Through the debacle of Election 2000…through the tragedy of September 11ᵗʰ and the ensuing war on terror…through the wars in Afghanistan and Iraq….He is calling to us! He is beseeching us, He is imploring us, as Mordechai besought and implored Esther — to recognize the times. **"Recognize your destiny!** See who you're married to. Go to Him! Join with Him in intercession for this hour, that deliverance might come, for **you have been born for such a time as this!"**

OUR CALLING

Our God indeed calls us to seek Him as did Hezekiah and Judah; as did Mordechai and Esther. I believe with all my heart that if we do, that door of mercy will become not just an open door, but an "open heaven" over our land. We will see revival and awakening, reformation and transformation. I have faith to believe that another fulfillment of God's redemptive purpose, in all its aspects, is possible for our nation. Do you have faith to believe this? Though we are threatened from within and without, we must press into the presence of God and cry out to Him, just as Hezekiah and Esther did in times of great national crisis.

I believe God has callings for nations, for peoples, and for cultures, as well as for individuals. It is our great privilege and unique joy to find what our God-ordained purpose is, and to fulfill it. Over the life of every individual, as well as every nation, there rages a cosmic battle. The spiritual warfare is very real. The stakes are high; the battle is intense. The histories of lives, of countries, of generations, testify to this battle. Consider the lives examined in this book. Consider Esther. Or Hezekiah. Or Moses. Consider our founding grandfathers, the Pilgrims and the Puritans.

OUR RESPONSE

I truly believe a fresh victory can be ours, but only through abject dependence on the Master Weaver. In these momentous days in which we live, we need to look at our lives, the Church, and the nation through the eyes of the Master Weaver. We need to see what He sees. We need to take a spiritual inventory of our lives, as well as of the Church and the nation. We need to invite the Lord to clean house.

What does the Lord ask of us at this hour? First and foremost, He asks us to live lives of **repentance.** The Christian life begins with repentance and faith. The Lord never designed for us to become Christians and then forsake the path of repentance and faith! That is what our sanctification is about: walking more intimately with Jesus, so that we become aware of that which offends and grieves Him. We then repent, and lay it down. The Lord commands us to repent. He commands us to get the rubbish out of our temples. He commands us to consecrate ourselves to the Lord.

The Lord wants us to live a lifestyle of repentance as long as we walk this earth. If we do not, we will become stagnant, and we will soon forget the Cross. We will forget how powerful and beautiful mercy and grace are. If we are not in touch with our sin, then mercy and grace do not mean very much. But if I have a fresh understanding of how I sinned today, then the fountain of mercy and grace that bubbles up from the Cross is beautiful. It is life-giving, and it quenches our thirst, a thirst that we realize we have for the mercy and grace of God, and for nothing else. Yes, out of His perfect goodness, God calls us to repent. Not just as the Church, but as Americans.

How about you? How will you respond to the Lord in this hour? Will you live a life of repentance before the Lord? Will you ask the Lord, "Give me a holy fear of You?" We have so abused grace in our culture that we do not fear the Lord anymore. Will you repent?

Will you ask for a holy fear of the Lord? Will you ask for an undivided heart (Psalm 86:11)? A heart committed to the kingdom of God and the house of God, above any other earthly treasure?

Will you **commit to pray** every day for revival in your life, in your family, and in your church? People talk a lot about revival, but what is revival? I believe revival comes when the Holy Spirit gives us such a revelation of the holiness of God that we are undone, as Isaiah was! (Isaiah 6:1-8). How we, too, need the touch of that tong from the altar of God. When we receive that touch, we are so impassioned by gratitude and worship, that we cry out, like Isaiah, "Here am I, send me!" We are filled with a passionate desire to be doing whatever it is that God is doing in our day. Everything else grows strangely dim as we recognize what the battle of our age is, as we recognize what the unique struggle of our generation is! We want to give ourselves to it!

Will you **pray for revival** in your own life, and in the Church of this nation? Will you pray daily for a spiritual awakening in America? Such a commitment to prayer will change your life, and you will never regret it! This prayer has revolutionized my life, and I continue to cry out to God for revival and spiritual awakening every day.

Would you consider not only praying for revival and awakening, but also, as the Lord leads you, learning **to fast** and pray? Fasting is a lost discipline. O, that the Lord would revive it in this needy hour. Many believers have begun to fast every Friday, beseeching the Lord for a move of God in our country and around the world. Some of us, for health reasons, might not be able to fast from food, but we can fast from other things. We can fast from amusements; perhaps movies, television, or sports. We can fast from whatever it is that means something to us personally. We need to learn to fast and pray because, as I've noted throughout this book, fasting and prayer bring the breakthrough. A spirit of fasting and prayer is what will bring about our much-needed deliverance in this hour.

I believe this is God's word to us, today:

'God opposes the proud, but gives grace to the humble.'

Submit yourselves, then, to God. Resist the devil, and he will flee from you. Come near to God and he will come near to you. Wash your hands, you sinners [He is writing to believers, now!], and purify your hearts, you double-minded. Grieve, mourn and wail. Change your laughter to mourning and your joy to gloom. Humble yourselves before the Lord, and he will lift you up. (James 4:6b-10)

Jesus Himself said, "Blessed are those who mourn, for they will be comforted." (Matthew 5:4) God calls us **to mourn.** Do you know why? Because, I believe, that as He intercedes for us, Jesus Himself mourns! If He mourned for the Jews, and if He wept over Jerusalem, do you think He does not mourn for our desperate state? Do you think that He would not weep for us? If Jesus weeps because He is so deeply grieved, should we not weep also?

Will you pray and ask God to grieve your heart with what grieves His? To break your heart with what breaks His? Will you ask the Lord to give you His tears, the tears of the Lord, expressed in a heartbroken prayer, a heart-cry for revival and awakening?

If we so respond, then I believe we can ask our Master Weaver to take that scarlet thread of the redemptive purpose of this nation, as frayed and as discolored as it is, and to restore it to a new brilliance. Praise God that it is on His heart to show us mercy, and to weave all of our lives together into the tapestry that is the kingdom history of this generation. Our tableau is connected to all those preceding it, and all those that may follow. This, however, is our moment! My life is a thread, and your life is a thread. God can weave them together into a tapestry that is larger, greater, more diverse, more unified, and more awe-inspiring than any that He has yet displayed in the gallery of our history.

Such a tapestry would be the tapestry of a Fourth Great Awakening in our nation. An awakening with the potential to touch and transform the nation, as did the revival in Hezekiah's day. An awakening with the potential to bless Israel and the Jewish people, as Cyrus did. An awakening, the result of which would be the power, through dependence upon God, to repel the aggressive onslaught of Islamic fundamentalism. Do you see how important this is? For our nation, for Israel and the Jewish people, for the world, and for civilization as we know it!

I believe we face a crisis even greater than that which Esther faced. Greater than what Hezekiah faced. But if we look to their example, and respond as they did, then I believe with all my heart that God will hear us. Our role is to cry out with Daniel, "O Lord, listen! O Lord, forgive! **O Lord, hear and act!** For Your sake, O my God, do not delay, because your city and your people bear your Name" (Daniel 9:19).

A PRAYER FOR AMERICA

I would like to close this book with a prayer that was written by William Penn, the founder of the colony of Pennsylvania. Penn, an atheist, was converted in England, and then imprisoned at least twice for sharing his faith in England. He came to the New World in order to found Pennsylvania. He dreamed that it would be a haven for those seeking refuge from religious persecution.

To more meaningfully set the stage for Penn's prayer, let me first relate what I experienced in Washington, DC, in the early morning hours of September 11, 2001. The night before that momentous day, the Lord spoke to me through a dream, *"Virgin daughter Jerusalem; Virgin daughter Judah. As Jerusalem is to Judah, so Washington, D.C. is to America. Just as Jerusalem and Judah prostituted themselves and became a whore, so Washington, DC and the United States have prostituted themselves and become a whore. But I still see her as my virgin daughter, and I long to restore her."*

We have become a whore, a harlot. That is strong language, yet it is the language the Lord Himself uses over and over in the Old Testament, through his prophets. He uses very graphic language to portray the sins of His people. Yet, at the same time, there is hope. The Lord longs to restore us as His virgin daughter. When I later checked a concordance, I found to my surprise that the first Biblical mention of the phrase 'virgin daughter' was in reference to Jerusalem, in the day of...Hezekiah! (Isaiah 37:21-22)

The context was the overwhelming onslaught of Sennacherib, and the Lord's promised deliverance to His "Virgin Daughter of

Zion." Judah, the repentant whore, sought the Lord in great humility, and as a result, the Lord sent His mighty deliverance. I was absolutely awestruck as I received the Lord's message of hope from the Scriptures. I worshipped, overwhelmed with gratitude that we do indeed have a God who desires to speak to us today.

As Virgin Daughter America repents, she too can experience such a mighty deliverance. This is my prayer and my great hope.

I close now with the heartfelt prayer of William Penn, which he offered up for his beloved Philadelphia in 1684. May we make it our prayer for our nation as well:

> And Thou, Philadelphia *[Washington, DC, United States of America]*, the **Virgin** settlement of this province named before thou wert born. What love, what care, what service and what travail have there been to bring thee forth and preserve thee from such as would abuse and defile thee: O that thou mayest be kept from the evil that would overwhelm thee. That faithful to the God of thy mercies, in the Life of Righteousness [Jesus], thou mayest be preserved to the end. My soul prays to God for thee, that thou mayest stand in the day of trial, that thy children may be blest of the Lord and thy people saved by His Power.[132] [Emphasis Added]

A PRAYER IN RESPONSE

Our Heavenly Father, I pray that You would hear in our day the prayer of William Penn. In Your great mercy, would You hear it for our capital and our nation, in this desperate hour. Father, hear the prayers of our founding grandfathers, and the prayers of the remnant from that day to this. Forgive us for our failures! May we know them, that we may know You. May we know them, that we may know Your mercy and grace. Teach us to fear You, Lord. Restore us by Your Spirit to fulfill a unique and holy purpose, as individuals, as the Church, and as a nation. Father, I pray that You would grant us the conviction that we have been born for such a time as this. It is no coincidence that we live at this moment in history. Weave together the current tableau of Your tapestry of kingdom history.

Take the threads of our lives, Father, and weave them together, to fulfill Your holy purposes for us. Send an awakening that would not only bless our nation, but Israel and the Jewish people, as well as the nations of the earth. We beseech You to send an awakening that would save our world from the onslaught of the adversary in this hour. Father, we do not ask You these things because we deserve them; because we do not. We ask only because of the merits of Your great name. Have mercy on us, Father. Breathe on us again. We pray in Jesus' name, because it is for His glory that we desire to live and to pray, to worship and to serve. Amen.

Bibliography

Ali, Abdullah Yusuf. *The Holy Qur'an: Text Translation and Commentary*. Brentwood, MD: Amana Corporation, 1989.

Barnes, Fred. "Man with a Mission: George W. Bush Finds His Calling," *The Weekly Standard,* October 8, 2001, Vol. 007, Number 4.

Basler, Roy P., ed. *The Collected Works of Abraham Lincoln*. Piscataway, NJ: Rutgers University Press, 1990.

Bennett, Ramon. *Saga: Israel and the Demise of Nations*. Jerusalem: Arm of Salvation, 1993.

Beverley, James A. "Muhammad Amid the Faiths." *Christian History,* Issue 74 (Vol. XXI, No. 2).

Bonar, Andrew, ed. *Letters of Samuel Rutherford* (repr., Carlisle, PA: Banner of Truth Trust, 1984).

Bradford, William. *Of Plymouth Plantation*. New York: Random House (Modern College Library Editions), 1981.

Bright, Bill. *7 Basic Steps to Successful Fasting and Prayer*. (Booklet) Orlando, FL: NewLife Publications, 1995.

Bright, Bill. *The Coming Revival: America's Call to Fast, Pray, and*

Seek God's Face. Orlando, FL: NewLife Publications, 1995.

Brown, Michael L. *Our Hands Are Stained With Blood: The Tragic Story of the "Church" and the Jewish People.* Shippensburg, PA: Destiny Image, 1992.

Bush, George W. *A Charge to Keep.* New York: Morrow, 1999.

Cairns, Earle E. *Christianity Through the Centuries.* Grand Rapids, MI: Zondervan, 1981.

Cate, Dr. Patrick O. *Understanding and Responding to Islam: Insight on the September 11, 2001 Tragedy.* Dallas: Dallas Theological Seminary, 2001.

Coffman, Elesha. "Secrets of Islam's Success." *Christian History,* Issue 74 (Vol. XXI, No. 2).

Coolidge, Calvin. *The Price of Freedom: Speeches and Addresses.* New York: C. Scribner's Sons, 1924.

Crawford, Paul. "A Deadly Give and Take." *Christian History,* Issue 74 (Vol. XXI, No. 2), p. 20.

Elass, Mateen A. "Four Jihads." *Christian History,* Issue 74 (Vol. XXI, No. 2).

Finto, Don. *Your People Shall Be My People.* Ventura, CA: Regal, 2001.

Fisher, Dan. "A Region Reshaped 6-Day War: The Legacy of Conflict Series: THE SIX-DAY WAR: 20 Years AFTER" [sic]. *The Los Angeles Times*: May 31, 1987, page 1.

Hardman, Keith J., Ed. "Seasons of the Spirit," *Christian History,* Vol. VIII, No. 3, Issue 23.

Hexham, Irving, ed. *Concise Dictionary of Religion*, first published by InterVarsity Press, Carol Stream, USA, 1994; second edition, Regent College Press, Vancouver, 1999.

Irwin, David K. *What Christians Need to Know About Muslims.* (Booklet) Springfield, MO: Center for Ministry to Muslims, 1987.

Luther, Martin. *That Jesus Christ Was Born a Jew.* Reprinted in Talmage, Frank Ephraim, ed., *Disputation and Dialogue: Readings in the Jewish Christian Encounter.* New York: Ktav/Anti-Defamation League of B'nai B'rith, 1975.

Mansfield, Stephen. *The Faith of George W. Bush.* Lake Mary, FL: Charisma House, 2003.

Marshall, Peter, and Manuel, David. *The Light and the Glory.* Grand Rapids, MI: Fleming Revell, 1977.

McTernan, John, and Koenig, Bill. *Israel: The Blessing or the Curse.* Oklahoma City, OK: Heathstone Publishing, 2001.

Millard, Catherine. *Great American Statesmen and Heroes.* Camp Hill, PA: Horizon Books, 1995.

Morey, Robert. *The Islamic Invasion.* Eugene, OR: Harvest House, 1992.

Murray, Iain. *The Puritan Hope.* London: Banner of Truth Trust, 1971.

Packer, J.I., Tenney, Merrill C., and White, William Jr. *Illustrated Encyclopedia of Bible Facts.* Nashville, TN: Thomas Nelson, 1995.

Peterson, Merrill D., ed. *Thomas Jefferson: Writings.* New York: Literary Classics of the United States, 1984.

Prager, Dennis, and Telushkin, Joseph. *Why the Jews? The Reason for Antisemitism.* New York: Simon & Schuster, 1983.

Richards, Rob. *Has God Finished with Israel?* Milton Keynes, England: Word Publishing, 1994.

Tarr, Leslie K. "A Prayer Meeting that Lasted 100 Years." *Christian History,* Vol. I, Number 1.

Towns, Elmer. *The Beginner's Guide to Fasting.* Ann Arbor, MI: Vine Books (a division of Servant Publications), 2001.

Whan, Vorin E., ed. *A Soldier Speaks: Public Papers and Speeches of General of the Army Douglas MacArthur.* New York: Praeger, 1965.

Woodman, Ros. *The Great Celebration: A Puzzle Book About Hezekiah.* Ross-Shire, Scotland: Christian Focus Publications, 1995.

Woodward, Kenneth, and Gates, David. "How the Bible Made America." *Newsweek*, Vol. 100, Number 26 (December 27, 1982).

Endnotes

CHAPTER 1: AMERICA AT THE CROSSROADS

[1] Song, "Shout to the Lord," words by Darlene Zshech, from the album "Kiss of Heaven," © 2003, Integrity Music.

[2] Some readers may be offended by the fact that I believe that George W. Bush is a "leader according to mercy." Some may believe I am essentially saying that God is a Republican. In all honesty, that is not my intent. I am not interested in making a political statement, but rather a spiritual one. In integrity, I am bound to submit to you — the Body of Christ — what I believe the Lord has impressed upon my heart. I leave it to you, the reader, to "test" this statement as to whether it is from the Lord. (I John 4:1)

[3] Paraphrased from the worship song "Be the Center," words by Michael Frye. Vineyard Music, "Hungry."

[4] From the 8th-century Irish hymn, "Be Thou My Vision," translation by Mary E. Byrne, 1905. *Hymns for the Living Church*, Carol Stream, IL: Hope, 1974.

CHAPTER 2: STANDING IN THE GAP IN THE SPIRIT OF DANIEL, PART I

[5] Song, "When I Remember," from *He Chose the Nails*; words by Kim Hill and Jeff Silvey, performed by Kim Hill.

[6] Marshall, Peter, and Manuel, David, *The Light and the Glory*, Grand Rapids, MI: Fleming Revell, 1977, p. 216.

[7] *Ibid.*, 223-233.

CHAPTER 3: STANDING IN THE GAP IN THE SPIRIT OF DANIEL, PART II

[8] Bright, Bill, *7 Basic Steps to Successful Fasting and Prayer* (booklet), and *The Coming Revival: America's Call to Fast, Pray, and Seek God's Face,* Orlando, FL: NewLife Publications, 1995; and Towns, Elmer, *The Beginner's Guide to Fasting*, Ann Arbor, MI: Vine Books (a division of Servant Publications), 2001.

[9] From newsletter, "Generals of Intercession News," Vol. 9, No. 3, August/September 2000, page 5. Interested readers may contact Generals of Intercession at P.O. Box 49788, Colorado Springs, CO 80949-9788, or go to << www.generals.org >>

[10] Hymn, "When I Survey the Wondrous Cross," words by Isaac Watts, 1707. From *Hymns for the Living Church*, Carol Stream, IL: Hope, 1974.

CHAPTER 4: "ASK FOR THE ANCIENT PATHS"

[11] Bush, George W., *George W. Bush: A Charge to Keep*, New York: William Morrow and Co., 1999, pp. 8-9, 12-13.

[12] Bradford, William, *Of Plymouth Plantation*, New York: Random

House (Modern College Library Editions), 1981, p. 26.

[13] *Life of John Eliot, 7 (Lives of the Chief Fathers of New England, Vol. 3),* cited in Murray, Iain, *The Puritan Hope*, Banner of Truth Trust, 1971, pp. 92-93.

[14] Woodward, Kenneth, and Gates, David, "How the Bible Made America," *Newsweek*, Vol. 100, Number 26, pp. 44, 46.

[15] *Loc. cit.*

[16] *Ibid.,* p. 47.

[17] Peterson, Merrill D., ed., *Thomas Jefferson: Writings*, New York: Literary Classics of the United States, 1984, p. 518.

CHAPTER 5: REVIVAL AS IN THE DAYS OF HEZEKIAH

[18] Bradford, pp. 83-84.

[19] Marshall, pp. 161-162.

[20] *Ibid.,* p. 216.

[21] Edward Johnson, *The Wonder-Working Providences of Zion's Saviour in New England,* published in 1653; as quoted in Marshall, pp. 163-164.

[22] *The Great Celebration: A Puzzle Book About Hezekiah*, Ross-Shire, Scotland: Christian Focus Publications, 1995.

[23] From a collection of sermons by Stoddard, Solomon, titled *The Efficacy of the fear of Hell.* Printed in Boston by B. Green in 1713; quoted in *Christian History*, Volume VIII, Number 3, Issue 23, p. 10.

CHAPTER 6: GEORGE W. BUSH — A CHARGE TO KEEP

[24] Bush, George W., *A Charge to Keep*, New York: William Morrow & Co., 1999.

[25] Mansfield, Stephen, *The Faith of George W. Bush*, Lake Mary, FL: Charisma House, 2003, p. 11.

[26] *Ibid.*, p. 7.

[27] Barnes, Fred, "Man with a Mission: George W. Bush Finds His Calling," *The Weekly Standard*, October 8, 2001, Vol. 007, Number 4, p. 4; "Faith Guides Bush Through Era of Terror," interview with Don Evans, hosted by www.FoxNews.com, posted November 5, 2001.

[28] Bush, George W., p. 139.

[29] Words by Charles Wesley, 1762. From *Hymns for the Living Church*, Carol Stream, IL: Hope, 1974.

[30] "White House Staffers Gather for Bible Study," *USA Today*, October 13, 2002.

CHAPTER 7: IS GOD FINISHED WITH THE JEWISH PEOPLE?

[31] Richards, Rob, *Has God Finished with Israel?* Milton Keynes, England: Word Publishing, 1994, p. 54.

[32] Fisher, Dan, "A Region Reshaped 6-Day War: The Legacy of Conflict Series: The Six Day War: 20 Years After" [sic]. *Los Angeles Times*, May 31, 1987, page 1.

[33] "The New Rebel Cry: Jesus is Coming!" *Time* (June 21, 1971), p. 59.

[34] Finto, Don, *Your People Shall Be My People,* Ventura, CA: Regal, 2001, p. 127.

[35] *Ibid.,* p. 143.

[36] Thomas, Gary, "The Lord is Gathering His People," *Charisma,* (April 1997), p. 54.

[37] Thomas, Gary, "The Return of the Jewish Church," *Christianity Today* (September 1998), p. 63, as quoted in Finto, p. 143.

[38] Finto, p. 49.

[39] *Ibid.,* p. 43.

[40] *Loc. cit.*

[41] Murray, p. 256.

CHAPTER 8: THE 'RUTH' REMNANT OF THE CHURCH

[42] Richards, p. 23.

[43] Brown, Michael L., *Our Hands Are Stained With Blood: The Tragic Story of the "Church" and the Jewish People,* Shippensburg, PA: Destiny Image, 1992, p. 20.

[44] Finto, p. 39.

[45] Brown, p. 20.

[46] Bonar, Andrew, ed., *Letters of Samuel Rutherford* (reprint; Carlisle, PA: Banner of Truth, 1984), p. 599; quoted in Brown, p. 21.

CHAPTER 9: THE HISTORY OF THE CHURCH AND THE JEWISH PEOPLE: A BITTER LEGACY

[47] Finto, p. 88.

[48] *Ibid.*, p. 104.

[49] *Ibid.*, pp. 88-89.

[50] *Ibid.*, pp. 89-90.

[51] Brown, p. 10.

[52] *Ibid.*, pp. 10-11.

[53] Richards, p. 127.

[54] Brown, p. 12.

[55] *Loc. cit.*

[56] *Ibid.*, pp. 206-207.

[57] *Ibid.*, p. 60.

[58] Prager, Dennis, and Telushkin, Joseph, *Why the Jews? The Reason for Antisemitism*, New York: Simon & Schuster, 1983, p. 103, as quoted in Brown, p. 61.

[59] *Ibid.*, pp. 61-62.

[60] *Ibid.*, pp. 77-78.

[61] Luther, Martin, *That Jesus Christ Was Born a Jew,* reprinted in Talmage, Frank Ephraim, ed., *Disputation and Dialogue: Readings in the Jewish-Christian Encounter* (New York: Ktav/Anti-Defamation League of B'nai B'rith, 1975), p. 33,

quoted in Brown, p. 14.

[62] *Loc. cit.*

[63] Richards, p. 127.

[64] Brown, p. 12.

[65] *Ibid.,* p. 8.

[66] Interested readers can contact the International Christian Embassy of Jerusalem, P.O. Box 39255, Washington, DC 20016 USA, www.icej.org, or the Ebenezer Emergency Fund, P.O. Box 26, 162 Griggs Acres Road, Point Harbor, NC 27964-0026, www.operation-exodus.org.

CHAPTER 10: BLESSING OR CURSING?

[67] Richards, pp. 173-174.

[68] *Ibid.,* pp. 175-176.

[69] *Loc. cit.*

[70] *Loc. cit.*

[71] *Ibid.,* pp. 178-179.

[72] *Ibid.,* p. 176.

[73] McTernan, John, and Koenig, Bill, *Israel: The Blessing or the Curse*, Oklahoma City, OK: Heathstone Publishing, 2001, pp. 54-55.

[74] *Ibid.,* p. 56.

[75] *Ibid.,* p. 59.

[76] *Ibid.,* p. 64.

[77] *Ibid.,* pp. 71-72.

[78] *Ibid.,* pp. 161, 163.

[79] *Ibid.,* p. 82.

CHAPTER 11: THE TRUE FACE OF ISLAM

[80] Cate, Dr. Patrick O., *Understanding and Responding to Islam: Insight on the September 11, 2001 Tragedy,* Dallas: Dallas Thelological Seminary, 2001, p. 2.

[81] Irwin, David K. *What Christians Need to Know About Muslims* (Booklet) Springfield, MO: Center for Ministry to Muslims, 1987, p. 6.

[82] Morey, Robert, *The Islamic Invasion,* Eugene, OR: Harvest House, 1992, p. 6.

[83] Irwin, pp. 6-7.

[84] Morey, p. 5.

[85] Irwin, p. 6.

[86] *Ibid.,* p. 14-16.

[87] Elass, Mateen A., "Four Jihads," *Christian History,* Issue 74 (Vol. XXI, No. 2), pp. 35-36.

[88] *Ibid.,* p. 37.

[89] Cate, pp. 12-14.

[90] Elass, p. 38.

[91] Cate, p. 16.

[92] Beverley, James A., "Muhammad amid the Faiths," *Christian History,* Issue 74 (Vol. XXI, No. 2), p. 10.

[93] *Ibid.,* p. 12.

[94] *Ibid.,* pp. 13-15.

[95] Coffman, Elesha, "Secrets of Islam's Success," *Christian History,* Issue 74 (Vol. XXI, No. 2), pp. 17-18.

[96] Crawford, Paul, "A Deadly Give and Take," *Christian History,* Issue 74 (Vol. XXI, No. 2), p. 20.

[97] *Ibid.,* p. 23.

[98] *Ibid.,* pp. 23-24.

[99] "He [Khomeini] is conceivably the most important religious figure in the twentieth century because of the new confidence he has injected into Islam." Irving Hexham, ed., *Concise Dictionary of Religion*, first published by InterVarsity Press, Carol Stream, USA, 1994, second edition, Regent College Press, Vancouver, 1999.

[100] *Loc. cit.*

CHAPTER 12: THE CHURCH AND MILITANT ISLAM: KINGDOMS IN CONFLICT

[101] Missler, Chuck, tape series and accompanying notes, "The Sword of Allah," p. 3. Available from Koinonia House, P.O. Box

D, Coeur d'Alene, ID 83816.

[102] Morey, p. 52.

[103] Missler, p. 3.

[104] Morey, pp. 48-50, citing *The Encyclopedia of Islam, The Encyclopedia of Religion and Ethics, Encyclopedia Britannica, Encyclopedia of Religion,* and the *Encyclopedia of World Mythology and Legend.*

[105] *Ibid.,* p. 41.

[106] *Ibid.,* p. 82.

[107] *Ibid.,* pp. 42-43. Morey citing the following sources: Michael Nazar-Ali, *Islam: A Christian Perspective,* Philadelphia: Westminster Press, 1983, p. 21; Alfred Guillaume, *Islam,* London: Penguin Books, 1954, p. 6; Augustus H. Strong, *Systematic Theology,* Valley Forge: Judson Press, 1976, p. 186.

[108] Missler, p. 5, citing John McClintock, *Encyclopedia of Biblical, Theological, and Ecclesiastical Literature,* Grand Rapids, MI: Baker Books House, 1981 reprint, 6:406.

[109] *Ibid.,* p. 4.

[110] *Ibid.,* p. 7.

[111] *Ibid.,* p. 7, Missler citing: Dr. M. Baravmann, *The Spiritual Background of Early Islam,* Leiden: E.J. Brill, 1972; and Dr. Jane Smith, *An Historical and Semitic Study of the Term Islam as Seen in a Sequence of Quran Commentaries,* Univ. of Montana Press, for Harvard University Dissertations, 1970.

[112] *Ibid.,* p. 2.

113 Video, "The New Barbarians," by Caryl Matrisciana Productions, 30141 Antelope Road, Suite D228, Menifee, CA 92584.

114 Morey, p. 5.

115 Missler, p. 2.

116 Morey, pp. 20-22.

117 Missler, pp. 7-9. All the following quotes from the Qur'an are referenced on these pages in Missler. They are quoted from *The Holy Quran,* Yusuf Ali, translator (Brentwood, Maryland: Amana Corp., 1989).

118 Cairns, Earle E., *Christianity Through the Centuries: A History of the Christian Church,* Grand Rapids, MI: Zondervan, 1981, p. 185.

119 *Ibid.,* p. 200.

120 *Ibid.,* p. 180.

121 Tarr, Leslie K., "A Prayer Meeting that Lasted 100 Years," *Christian History,* Vol. I, Number 1, page 18.

122 Finto, p. 127.

123 Packer, J.I., Tenney, Merrill C., and White, William Jr., *Illustrated Encyclopedia of Bible Facts,* Nashville, TN: Thomas Nelson, 1995, p. 679.

124 Woodward and Gates, p. 44.

CHAPTER 13: FOR SUCH A TIME AS THIS

[125] Coolidge, Calvin, *The Price of Freedom: Speeches and Addresses*, New York: C. Scribner's Sons, 1924, pp. 331-353.

[126] Millard, Catherine, *Great American Statesmen and Heroes*, Camp Hill, PA: Horizon Books, 1995, p. 120.

[127] Speech delivered on April 3, 1951, at the laying of the corner-stone of New York Presbyterian Church. Source: Presidential Papers, Truman Presidential Library, Independence, Missouri.

[128] Steinbeck, in a letter to Adlai Stevenson, printed in the *Washington Post*, January 28, 1960.

[129] Basler, Roy P., ed., *The Collected Works of Abraham Lincoln.* Piscataway, NJ: Rutgers University Press, 1990.

[130] *Ibid..*, vol. 1, from speech delivered on January 27, 1837.

[131] Whan, Vorin E., ed., *A Soldier Speaks: Public Papers and Speeches of General of the Army Douglas MacArthur,* New York: Praeger, 1965, pp. 285-286.

[132] Millard, p. 56.

About the Author

Bill Lewis graduated *summa cum laude,* Phi Beta Kappa from Baylor University in 1984, and earned his M.A. from Grace Theological Seminary in 1987, studying under Dr. Larry Crabb.

He and his wife, Lynn, were missionaries in Russia for seven years, and then served in Israel for two years. They now live with their four children in Washington, DC.

Bill is the founder and president of Sons of Issachar Ministries, a ministry committed to helping Christians of our generation become like the Sons of Issachar, "who understood the times and knew what Israel should do" (I Chronicles 12:32). He shares this ministry vision with national leaders, and also speaks in churches as well as at conferences and retreats.

For information, or to inquire about speaking engagements, please contact Bill Lewis at:

Sons of Issachar Ministries, Inc.
P.O. Box 40913
Memphis, TN 38174-0913

www.SonsofIssachar.org

To order additional copies of this book, visit our website and click on the link to "Xulon Press."

Printed in the United States
60231LVS00006B/202